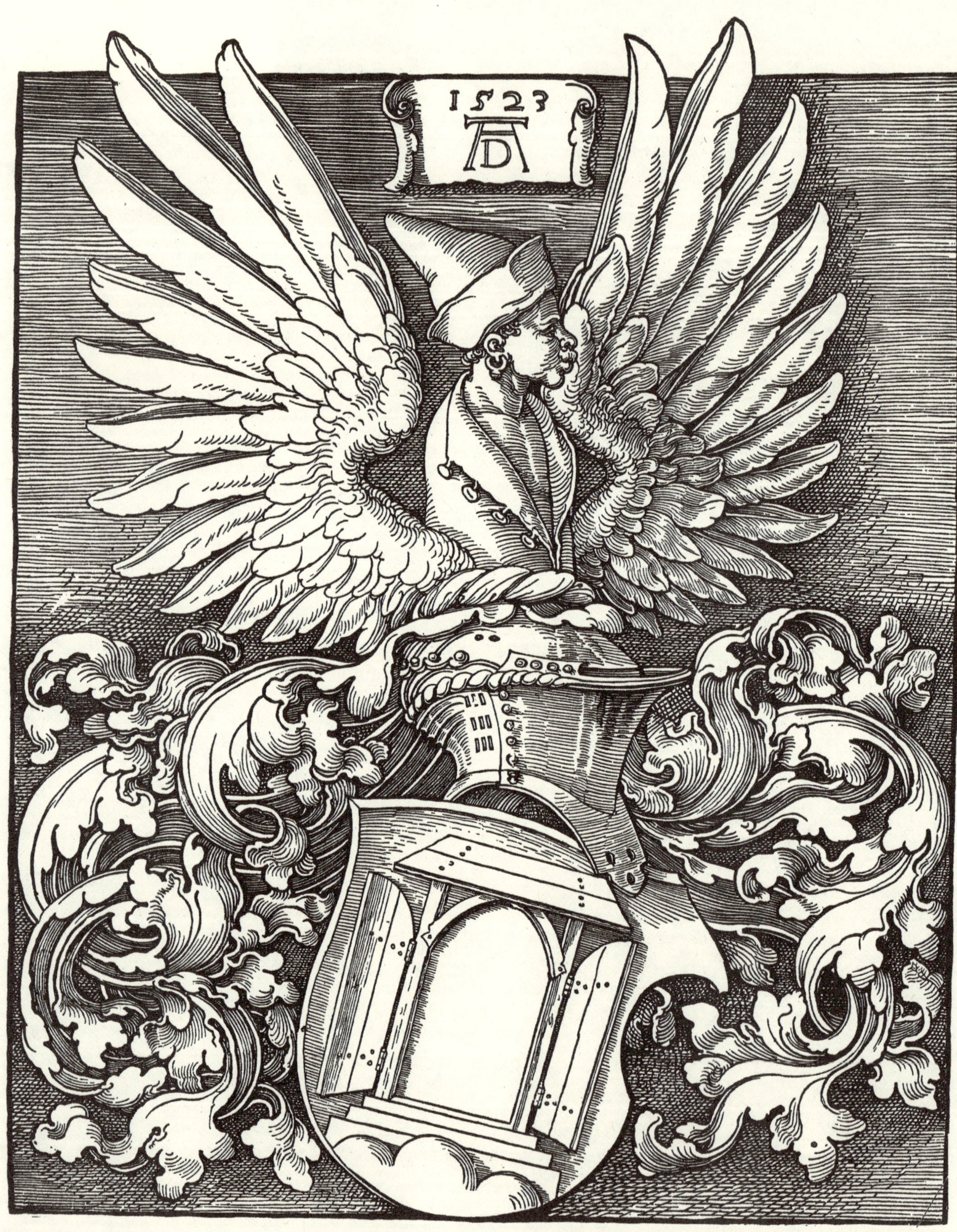

Dürer's Coat of Arms, 1523

Great Woodcuts of ALBRECHT DÜRER

94 ILLUSTRATIONS

Edited by
Carol Belanger Grafton

DOVER PUBLICATIONS
Garden City, New York

Bibliographical Note

This Dover edition, first published in 2004 and reissued in 2016, is a new selection of 94 plates from *The Complete Woodcuts of Albrecht Dürer*, originally published by W. & G. Foyle, Ltd., London, in 1927

DOVER *Pictorial Archive* SERIES

Library of Congress Cataloging-in-Publication Data

Dürer, Albrecht, 1471–1528.
[Completer woodcuts of Albrecht Dürer. Selections]
Great woodcuts of Albrecht Dürer / edited by Carol Belanger Grafton.—Dover ed.
p. cm. — (Dover pictorial archive series)
Originally published: The complete woodcuts of Albrecht Dürer. London: W. & G. Foyle, 1927.
"94 illustrations."
ISBN-13: 978-0-486-43401-8 (pbk.)
ISBN-10: 0-486-43401-X (pbk.)
1. Dürer, Albrecht, 1471–1528—Catalogs. I. Grafton, Carol Belanger. II. Title. III. Series.

NE11505.5.D8A4 2004
769.92—dc22

2003070048

Book design by Carol Belanger Grafton

Printed in Canada
43401X05 2025
www.doverpublications.com

NOTE

Producing over one thousand artistic masterpieces during his lifetime, Albrecht Dürer (1471–1528) was the first artist who elevated the graphic medium to an independent art form. Executed in a variety of techniques such as copperplate engravings, pencil drawings, woodcuts, and oil paintings, Dürer's vast body of work attained a precision of detail that has remained virtually unrivaled. The son of a goldsmith and jeweler, Dürer was trained as a draughtsman at a young age. He applied the same meticulous methods required in this delicate work to his woodcuts and engravings later on in his life. The precocious young painter and printmaker completed a remarkable self-portrait when he was just thirteen years old. In 1486 Dürer was apprenticed to the painter and woodcut illustrator Michael Wolgemut, whose workshop was considered to be the best in Europe. Having spent three years with Wolgemut, Dürer was now familiar with commercial bookmaking, and traveled to the Netherlands, Alsace, and to Switzerland, where he completed his first woodcut.

During his apprenticeship, Dürer had carefully studied the technique of woodcut illustrations. The high standards in the Wolgemut workshop inspired Dürer to develop his talent in this field. For woodcuts, Dürer simply provided sketches, which were then cut into the wood block by skilled artisans. In 1496 Dürer began work on a series of twelve woodcuts on the death of Christ, known as *The Large Passion,* a project that was to take him fifteen years to complete. His greatest printmaking achievement of his early years was the set of fifteen woodcuts on the revelations of St. John for the *Apocalypse* series (1498). These woodcuts display empathetic expression, rich emotion, and crowded compositions.

In 1494 Dürer married the daughter of a merchant. That autumn, he embarked on his first trip to Italy, where he remained until 1495. He would return there again in 1505–6. Several bold landscape watercolors—among Dürer's most beautiful creations—were completed there. His journeys to Italy had a strong impact on Dürer, and the influences of Italian painting resonated throughout his art for the next decade. A great admirer of Leonardo da Vinci, Dürer studied drawings and engravings that depicted the sinuous line of the human body in motion, and also became preoccupied with classical themes. From about 1500, Dürer's art clearly shows the effects of his intensive study of the mathematics of art. On his second sojourn to Italy, he delved even more deeply into the study of perspective and the mathematical theory of proportion by visiting the studios of other artists. Dürer continued to produce artwork of outstanding quality, including one of his most famous engravings, *Melancholia* (1514).

During the next several years, Dürer's health began to decline. Although he did not slacken his graphic work, he devoted nearly all his time and effort into his scientific and theoretical writings, among them the *Treatise on Proportion*. Completed in 1523, the book required an elementary knowledge of mathematics beyond what the average reader could be expected to have. Bearing that in mind, Dürer decided to write this basic text, which was published in four books in 1525 by his own publishing company. This treatise was the first book on mathematics published in German and places Dürer among the ranks of key Renaissance mathematicians. Even in his own day, Dürer was an internationally renowned artist with an impressive number of pupils and imitators. Reflecting back on Dürer, Florentine artist Giorgio Vasari referred to him as the "truly great painter and creator of the most beautiful copper engravings."

LIST OF ILLUSTRATIONS

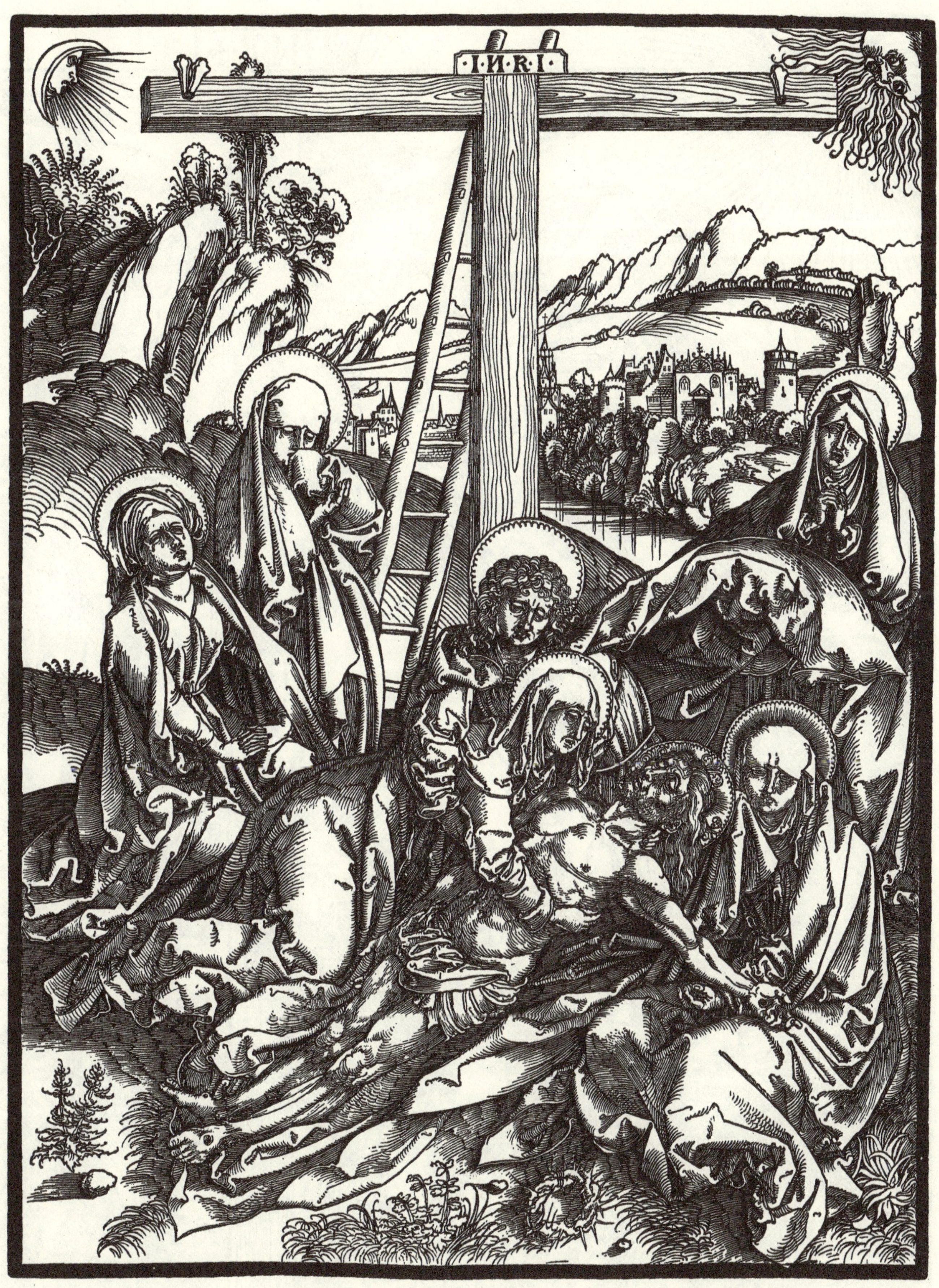

1. Lamentation for the Dead Christ

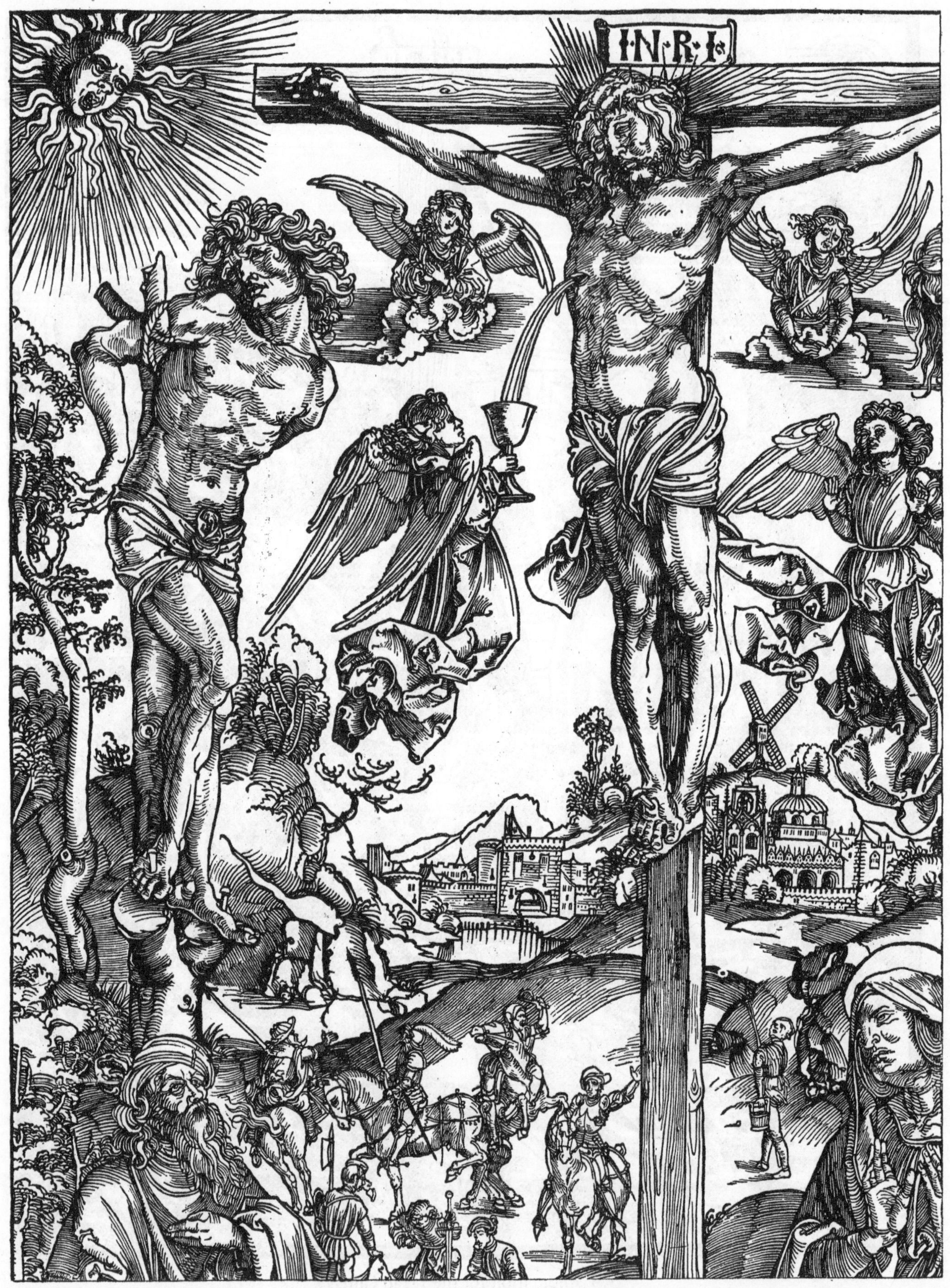

2. Crucifixion

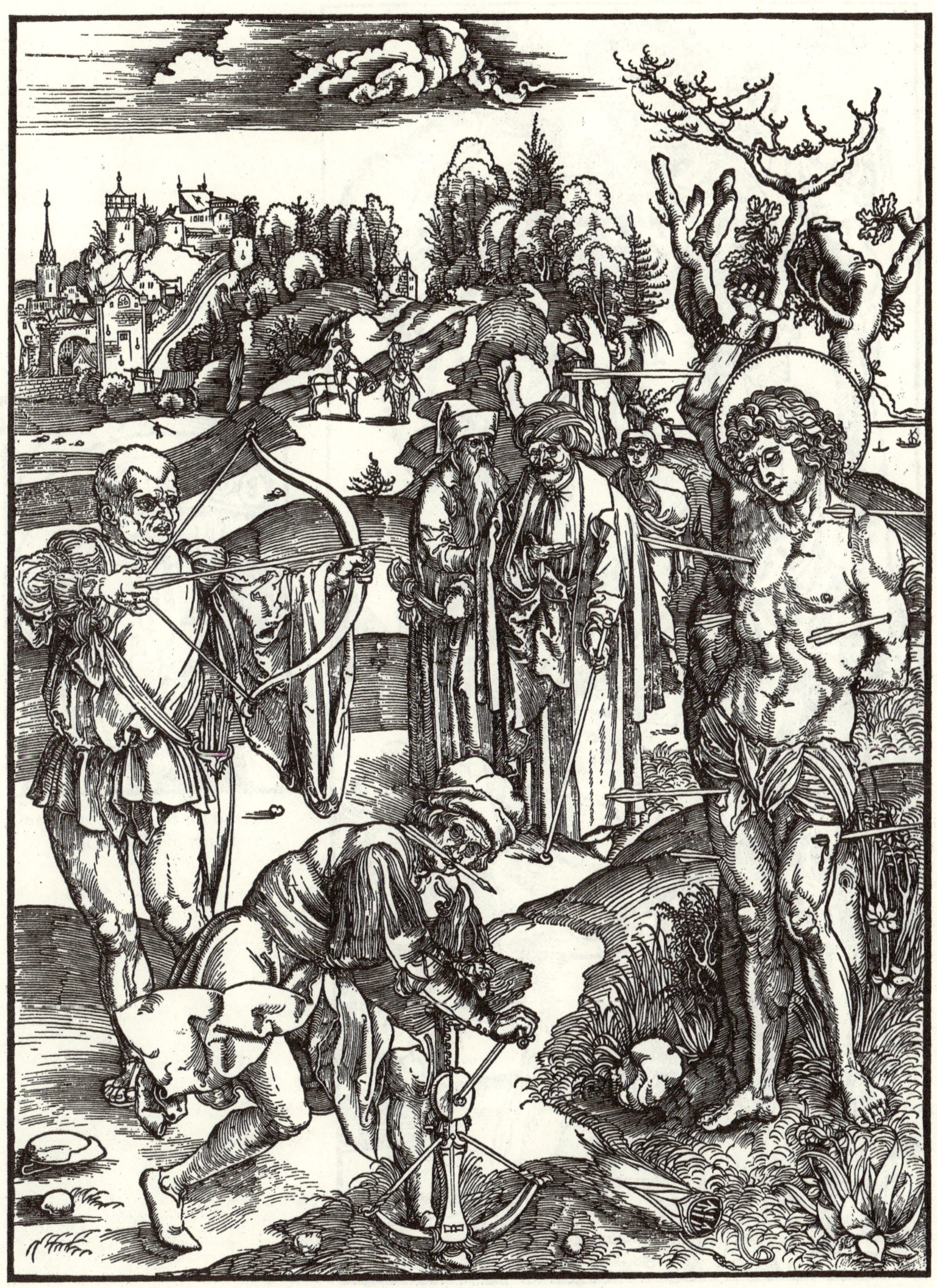

3. Martyrdom of S. Sebastian

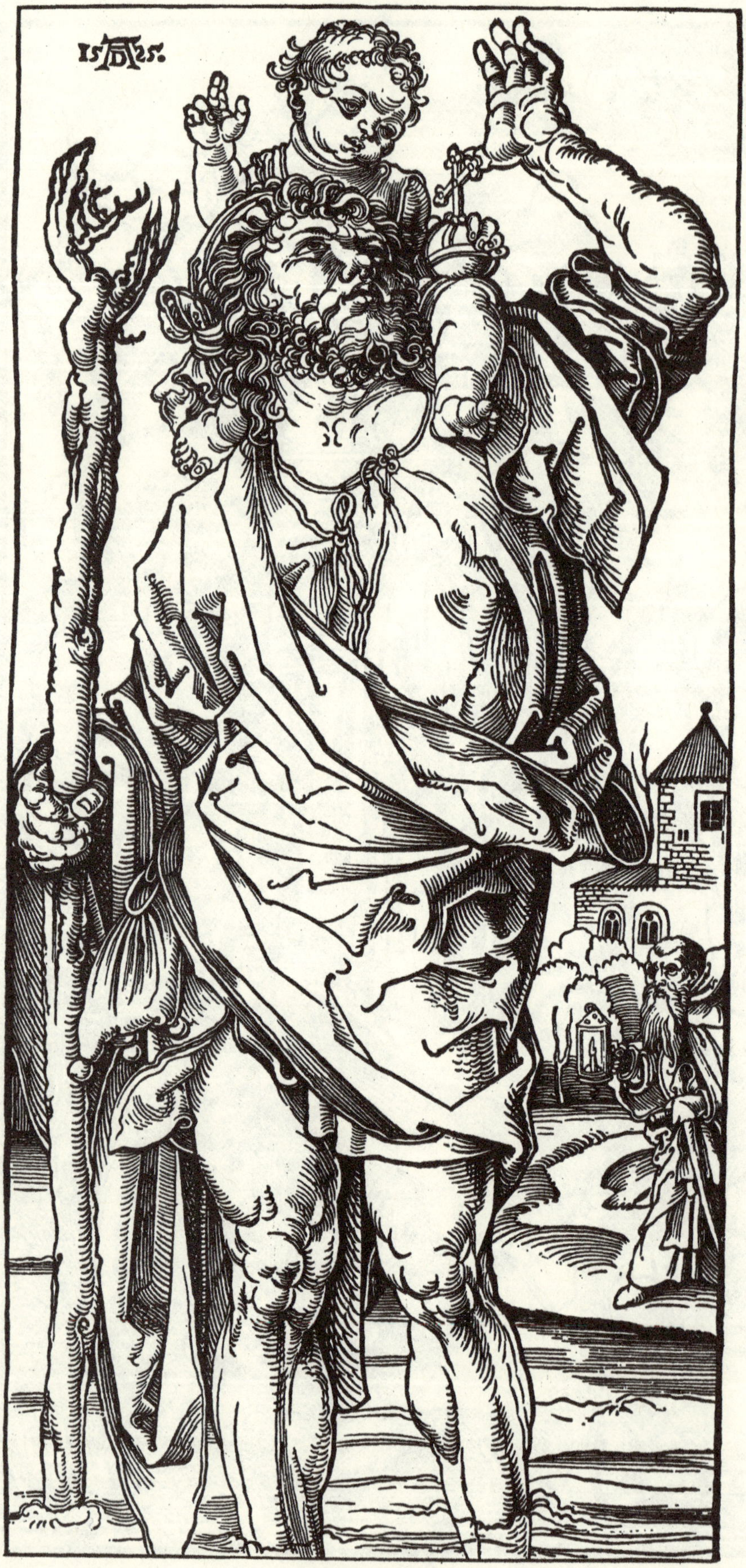

4. S. Christopher

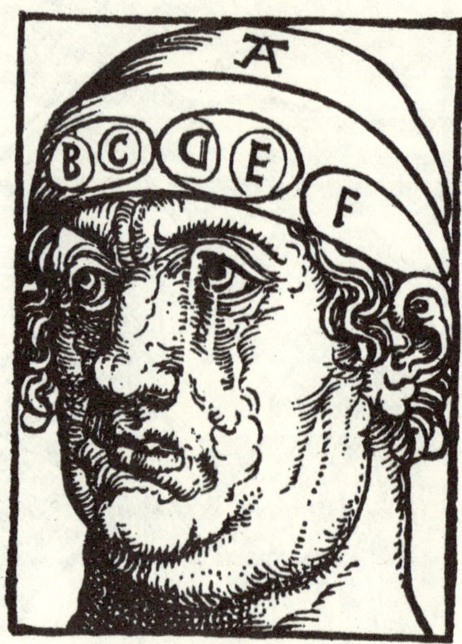

5. Head for the Purpose of the Study of Phrenology

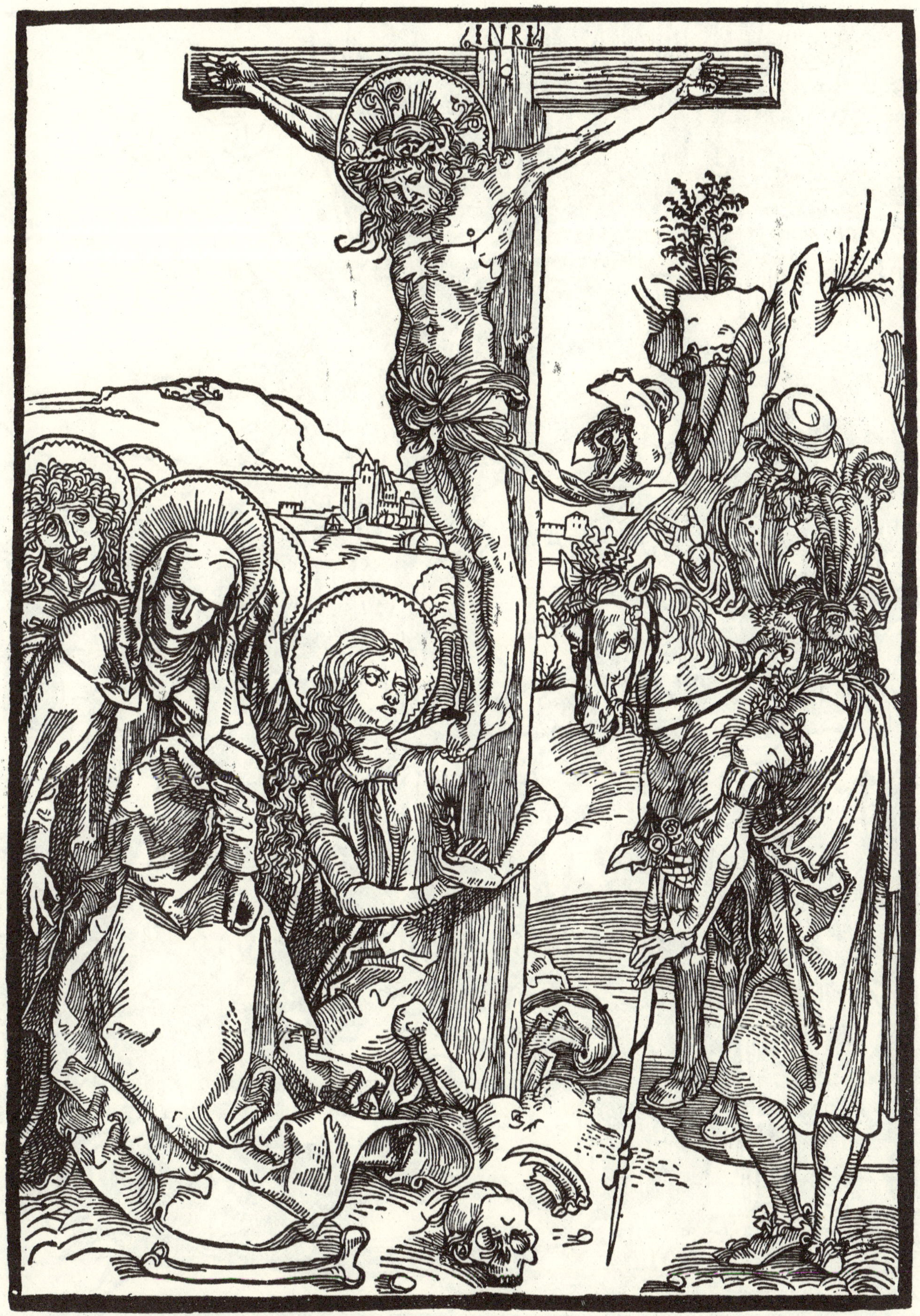

6. Crucifixion

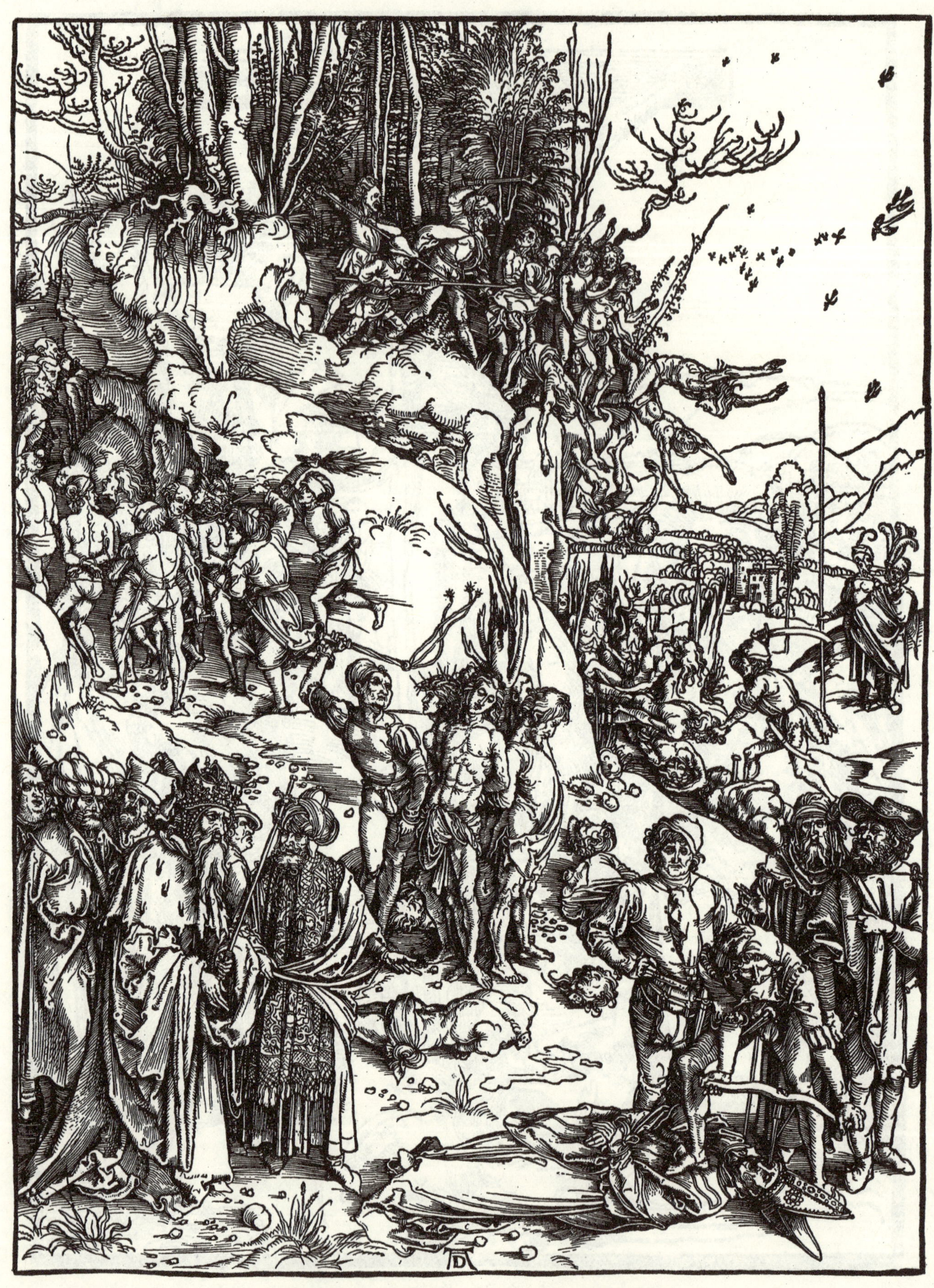

7. The Martyrdom of the Ten Thousand Christians

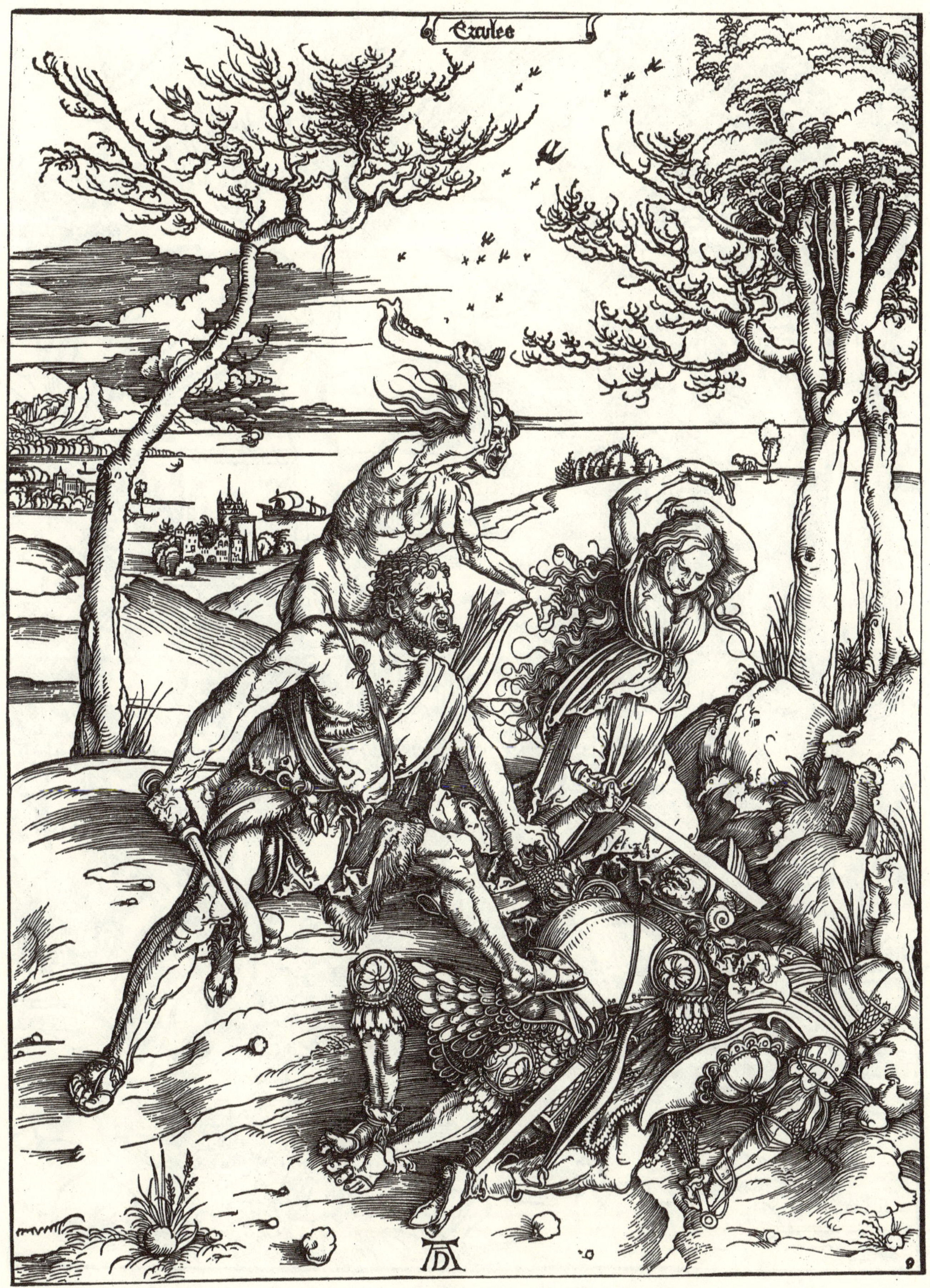

8. Hercules

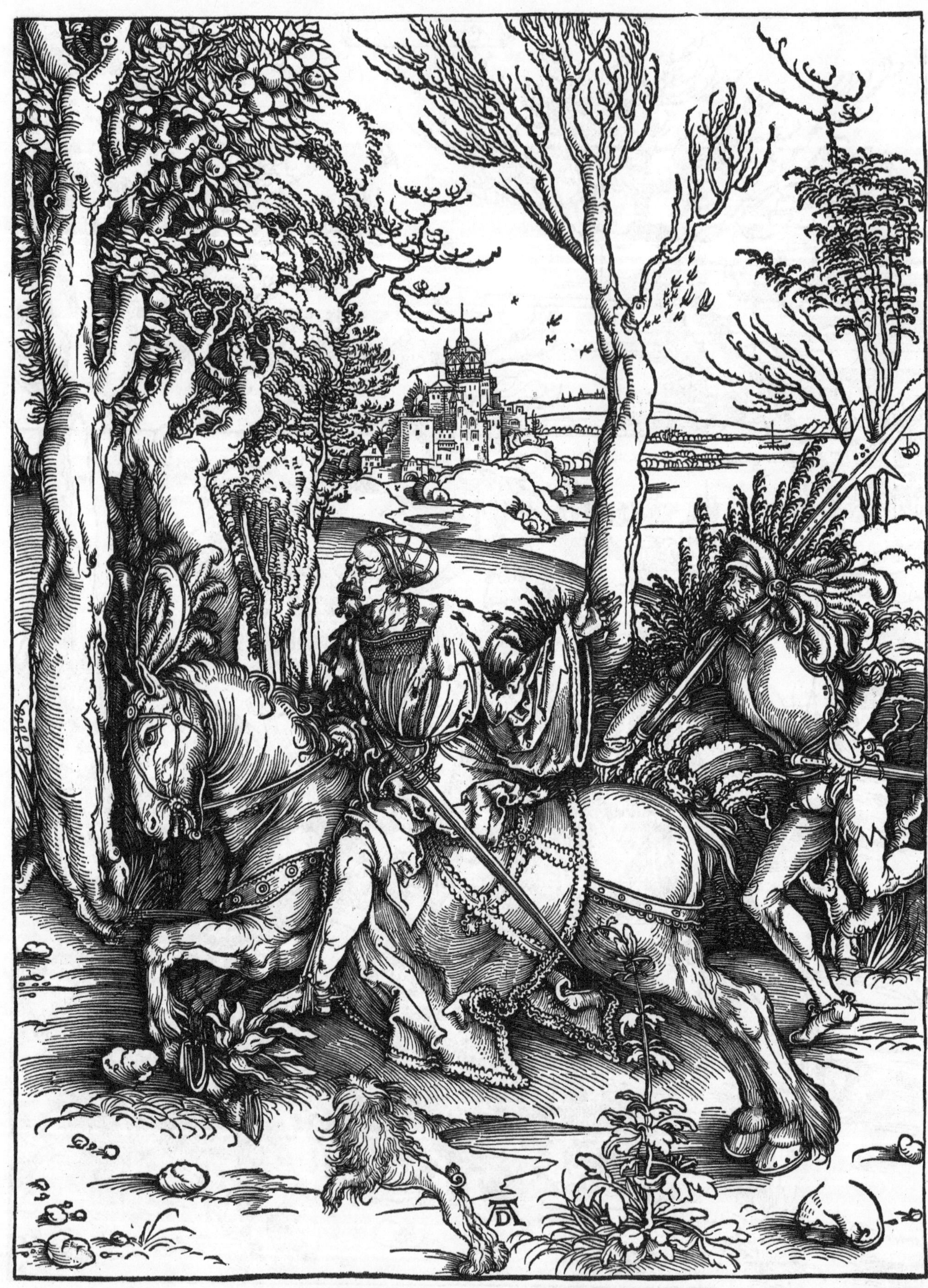

9. The Knight and the Landsknecht

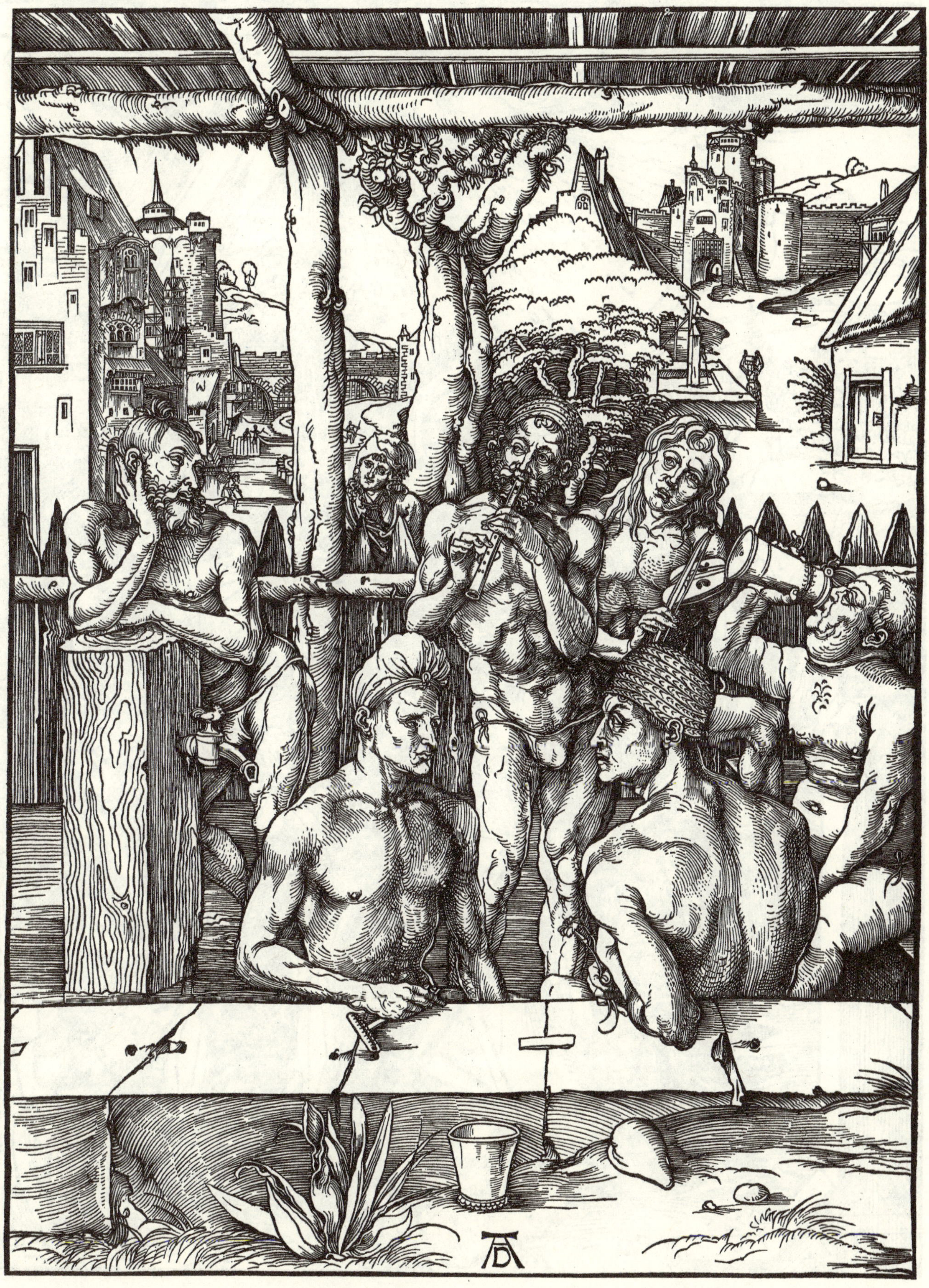

10. The Men's Bath

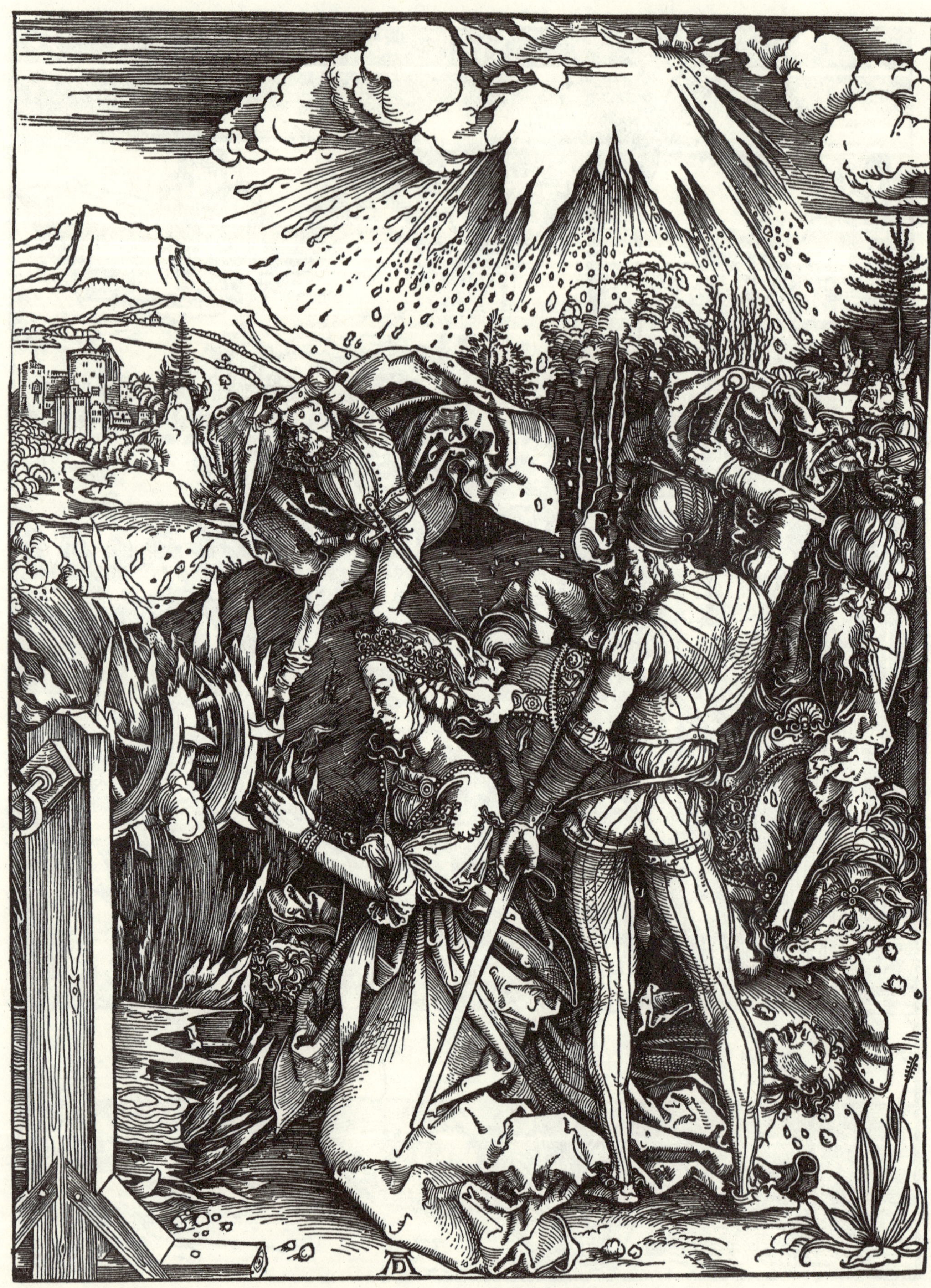

11. The Martyrdom of S. Catherine

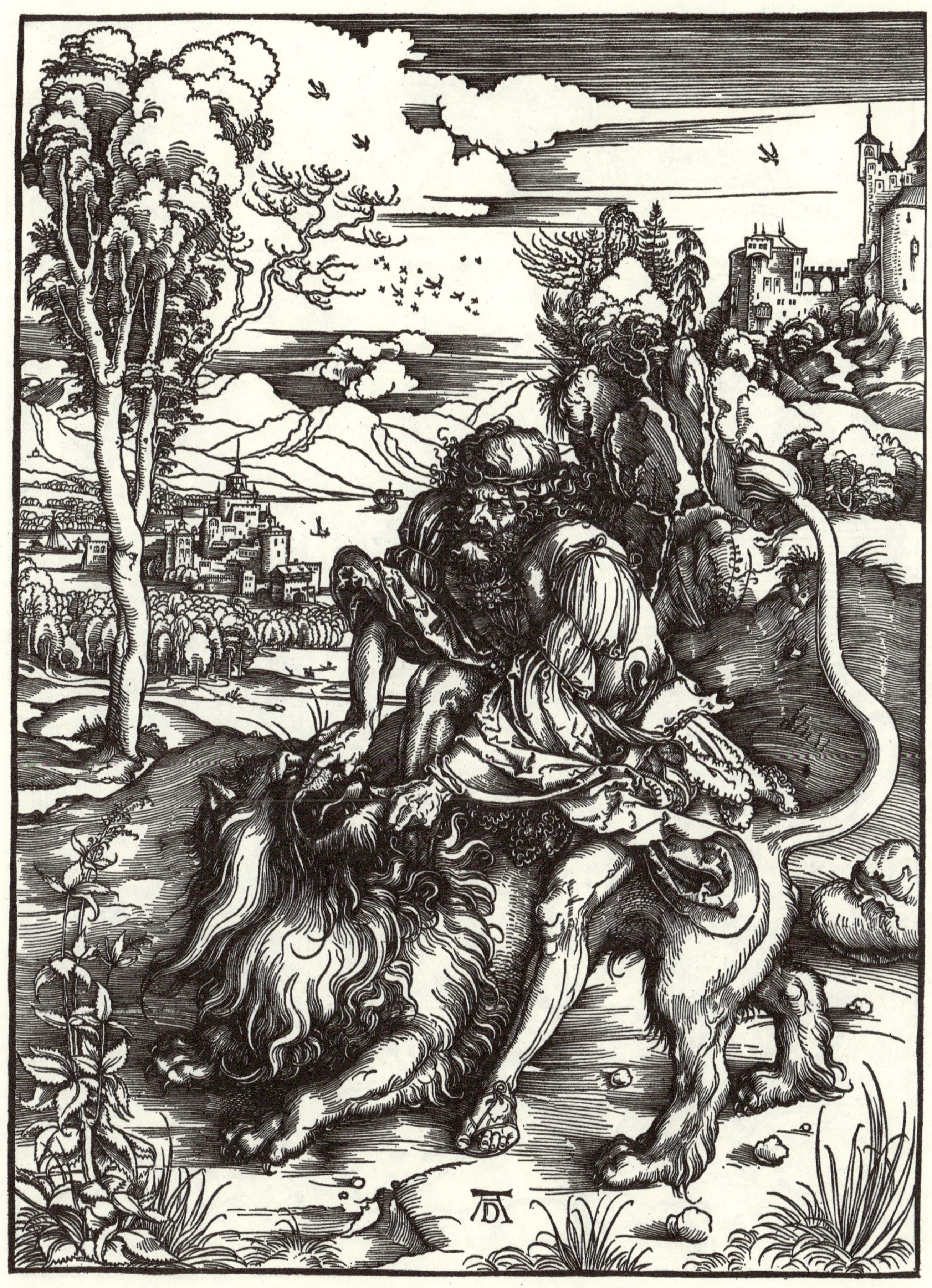

12. Samson Killing the Lion

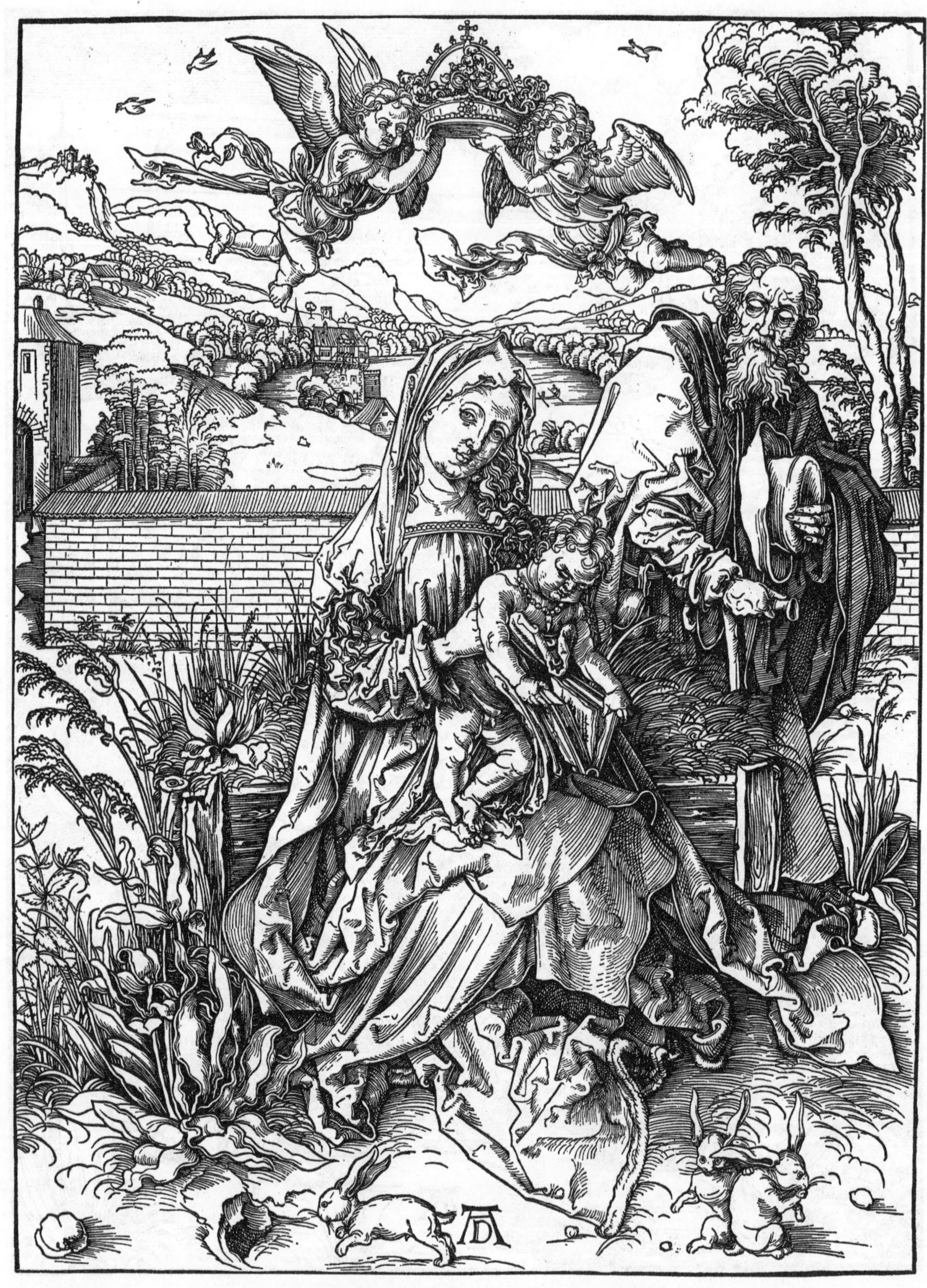

13. The Holy Family with Three Hares

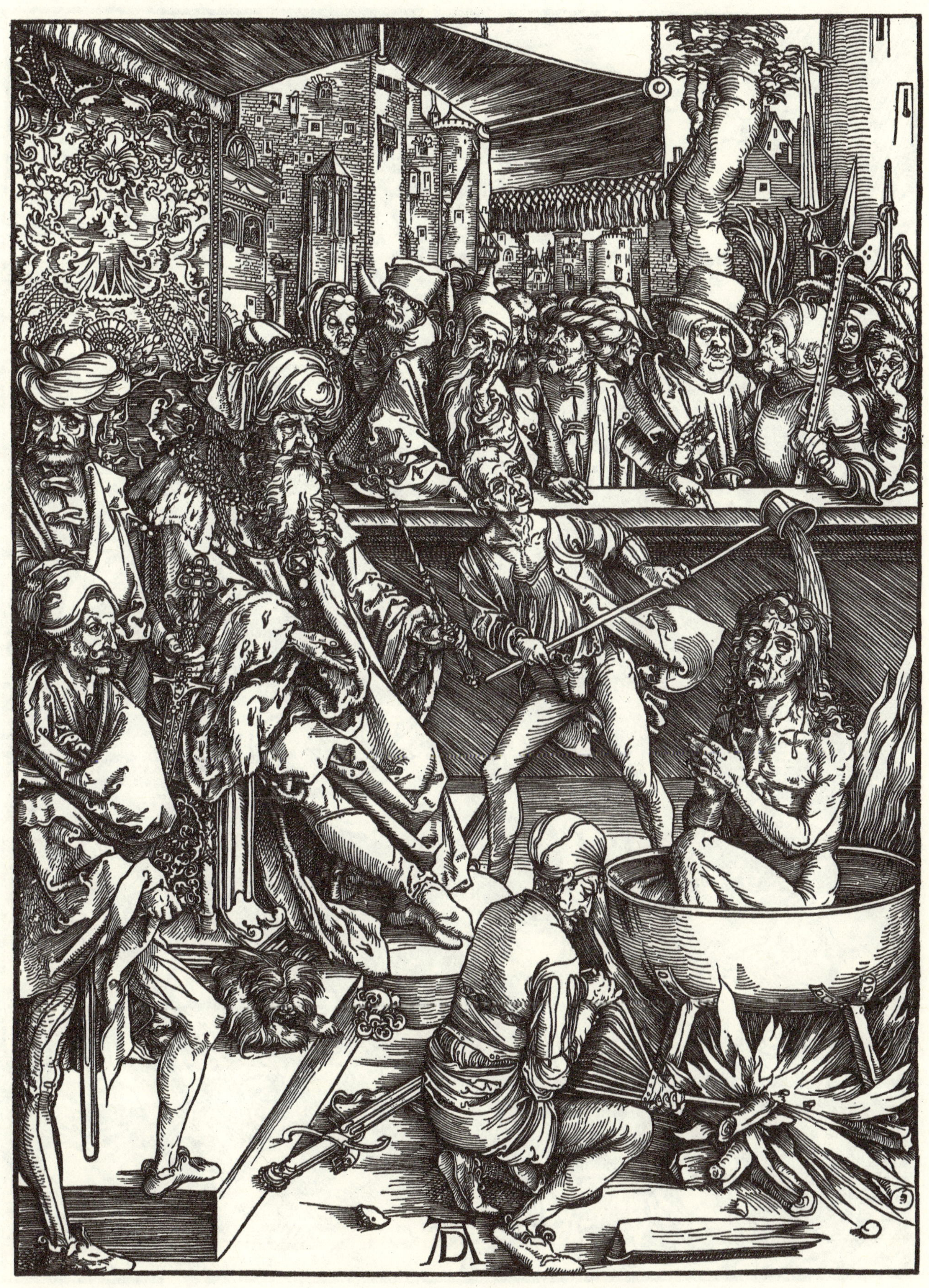

14. The Martyrdom of S. John the Evangelist

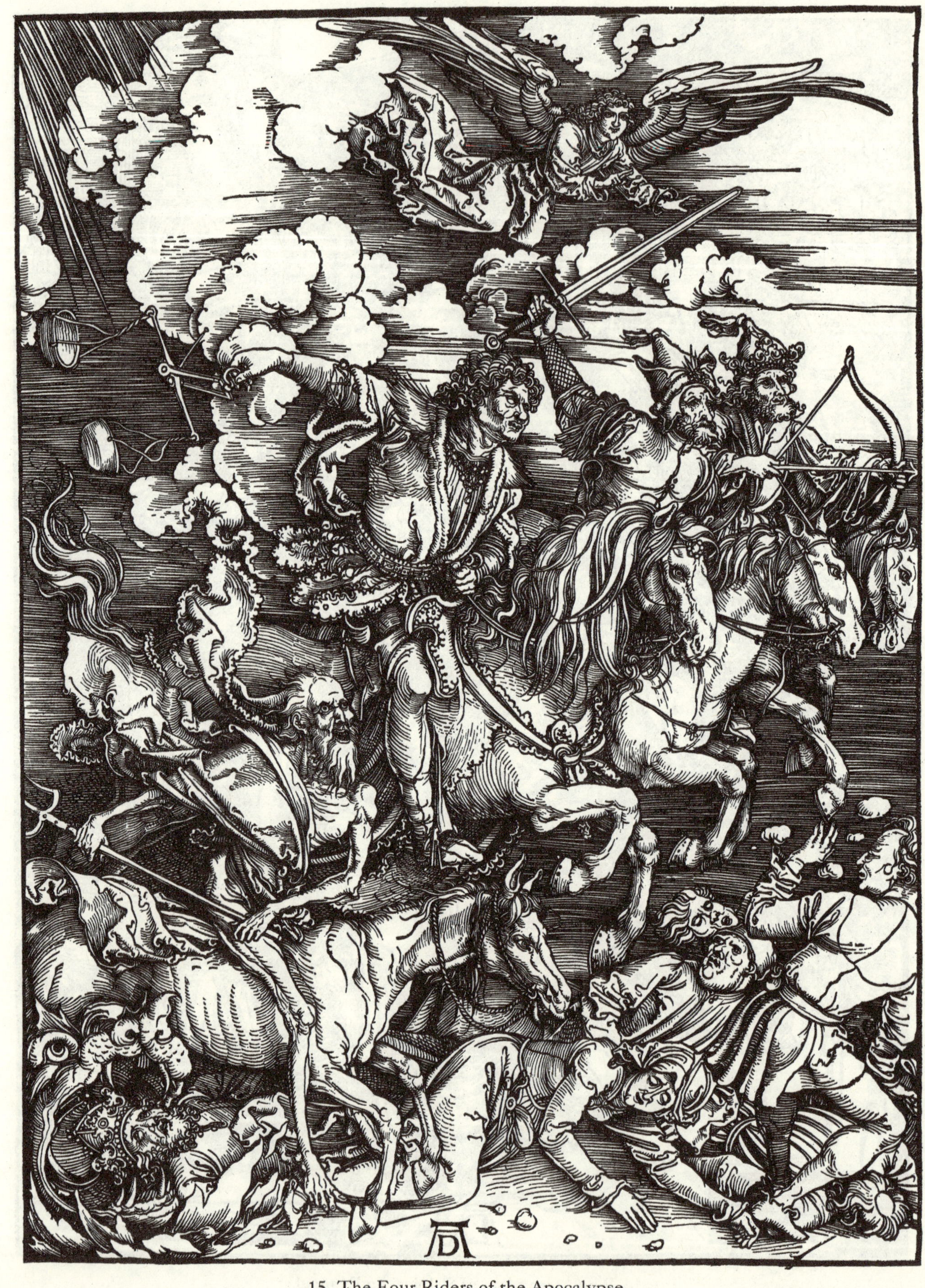

15. The Four Riders of the Apocalypse

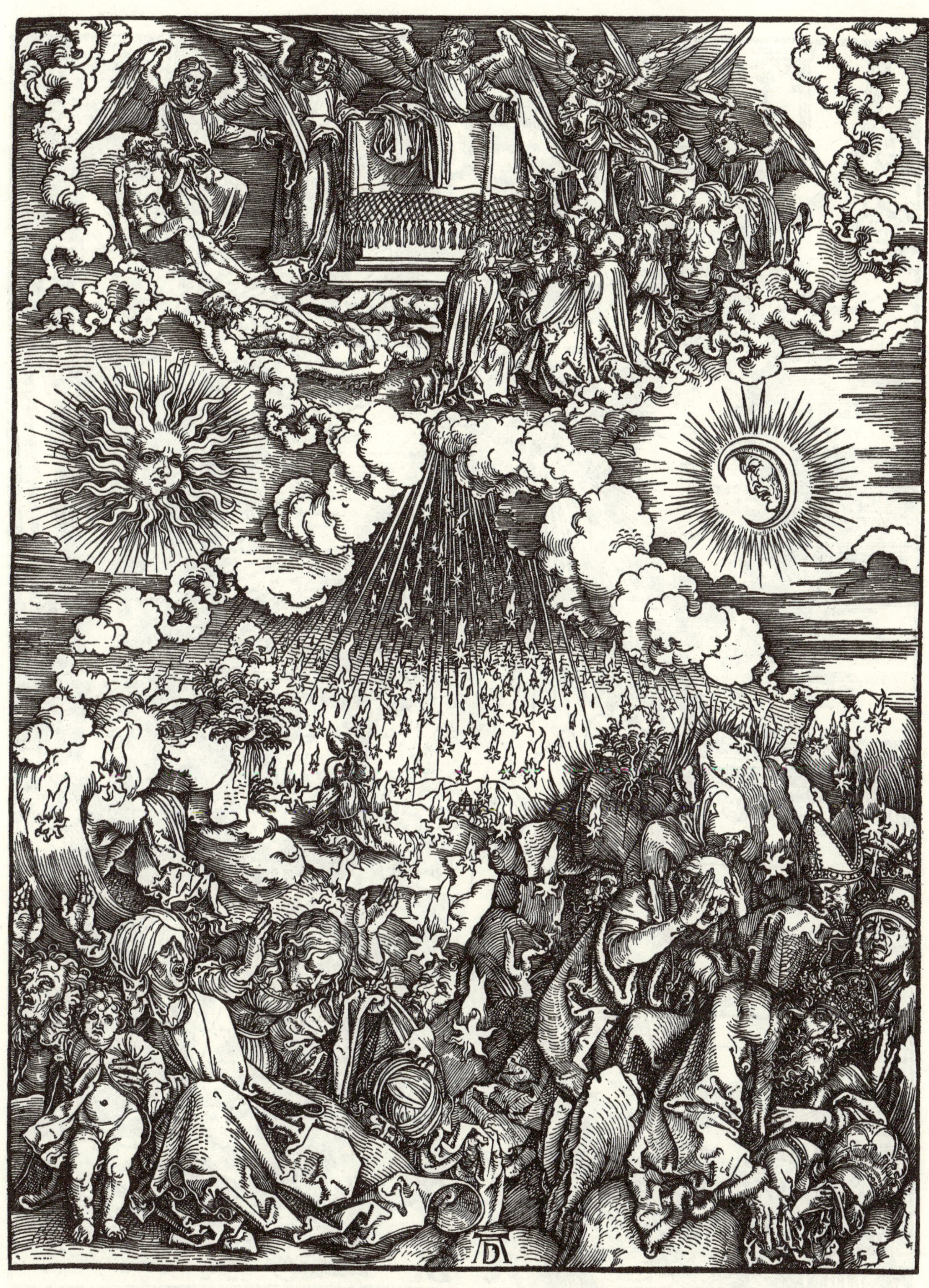

16. The Opening of the Fifth and Sixth Seals, the Distribution of White Garments Among the Martyrs and the Fall of the Stars

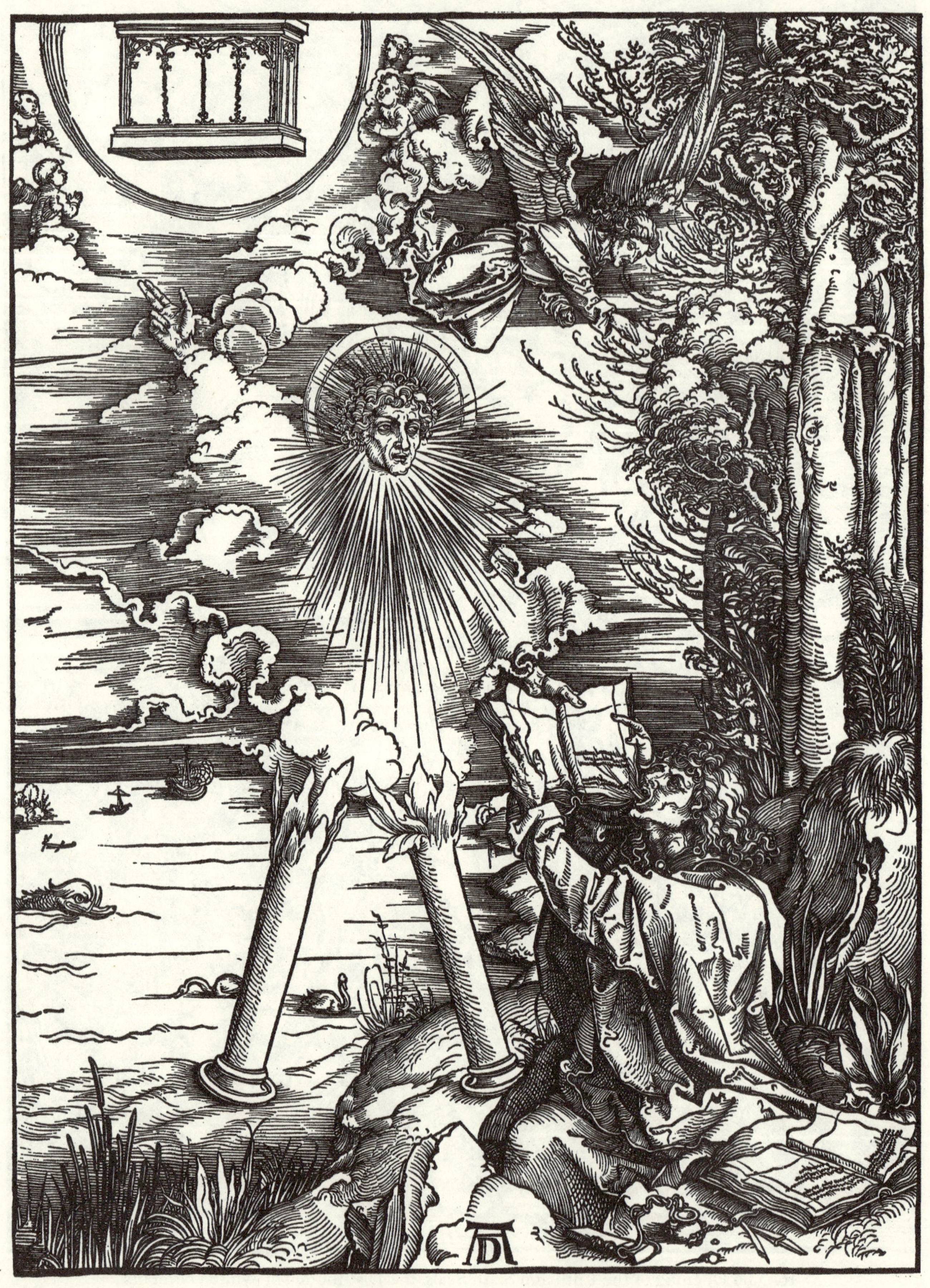

17. S. John Devours the Book

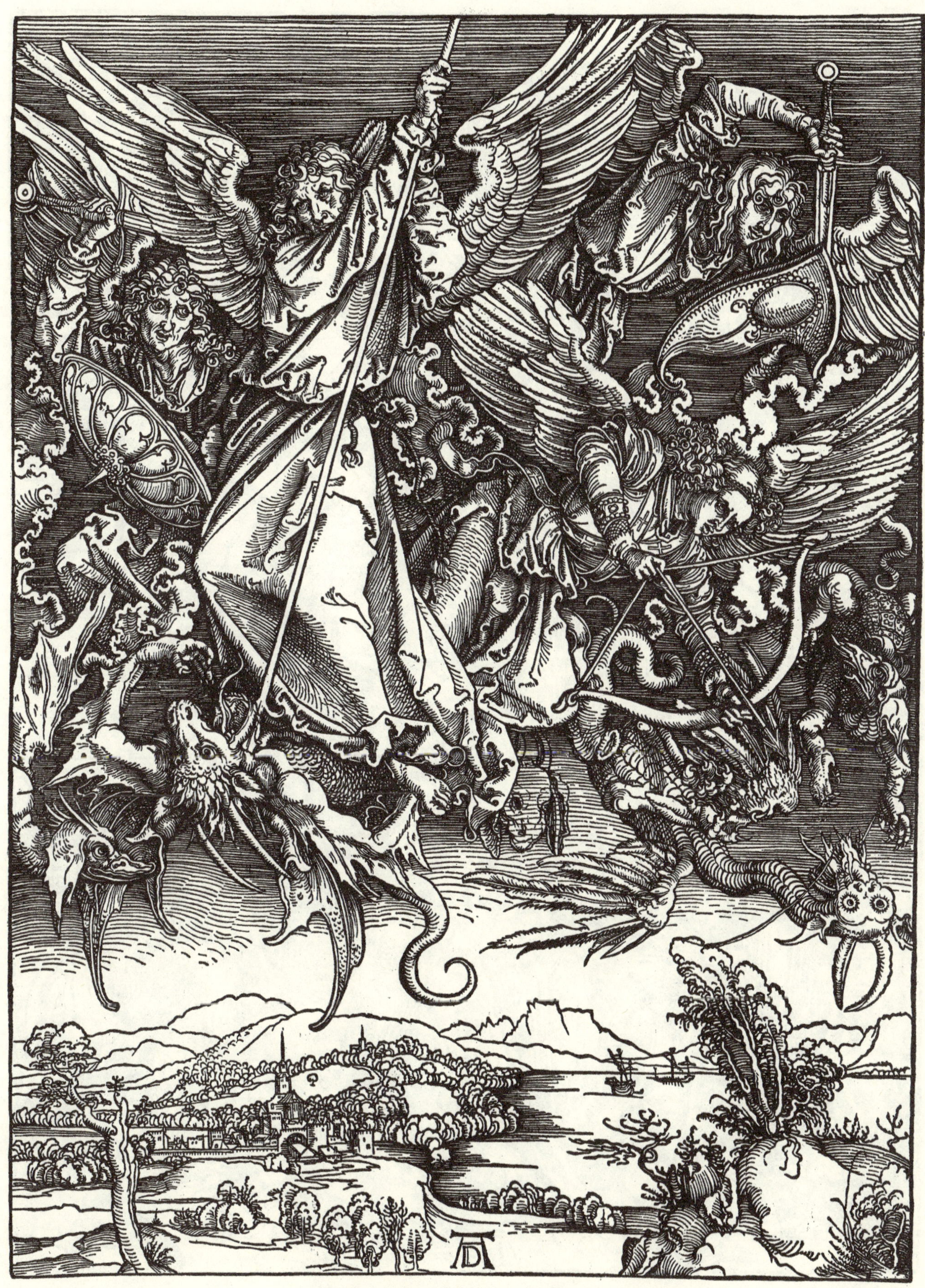

18. S. Michael Fighting the Dragon

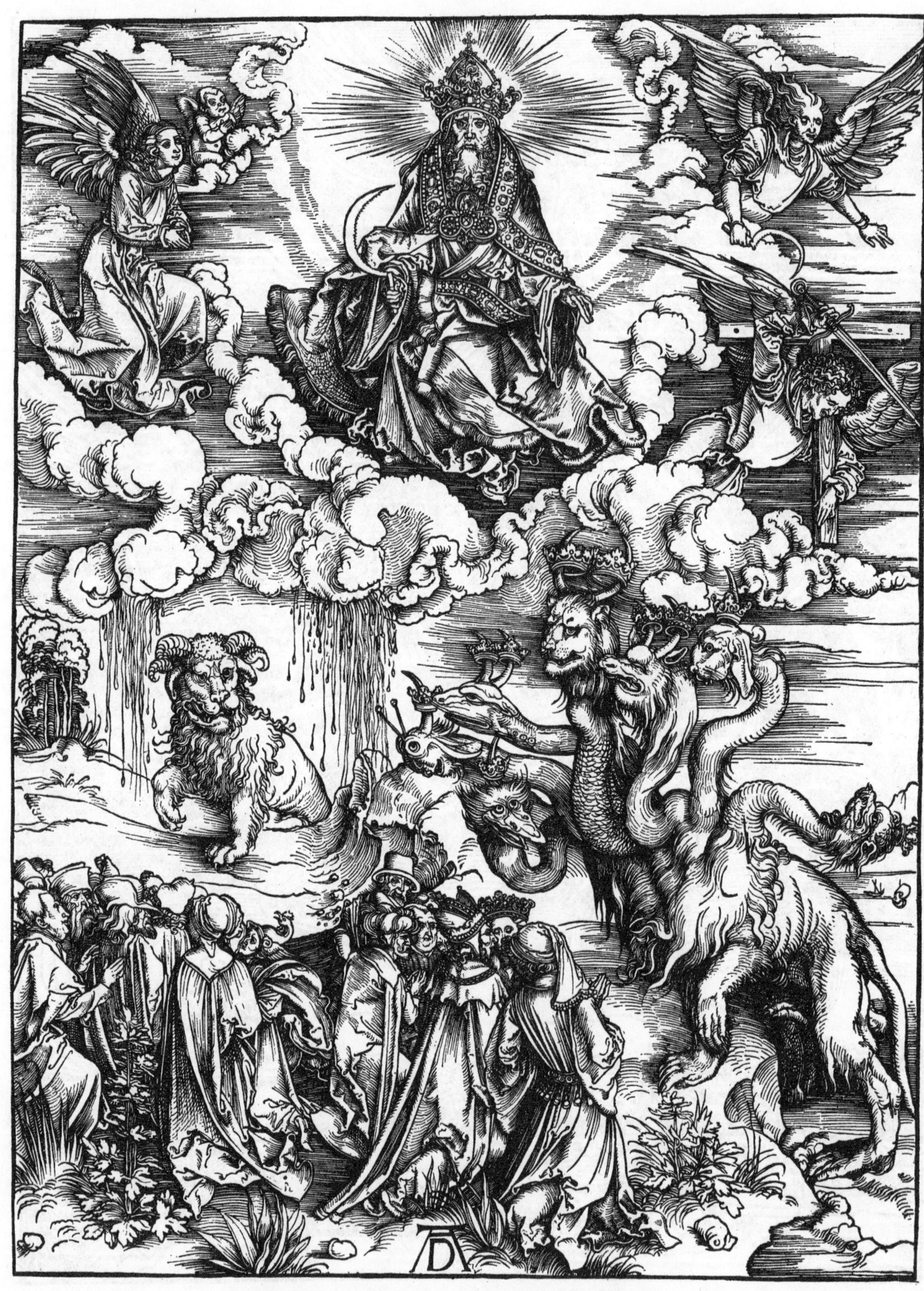

19. The Sea Monster and the Beast with the Lamb's Horns

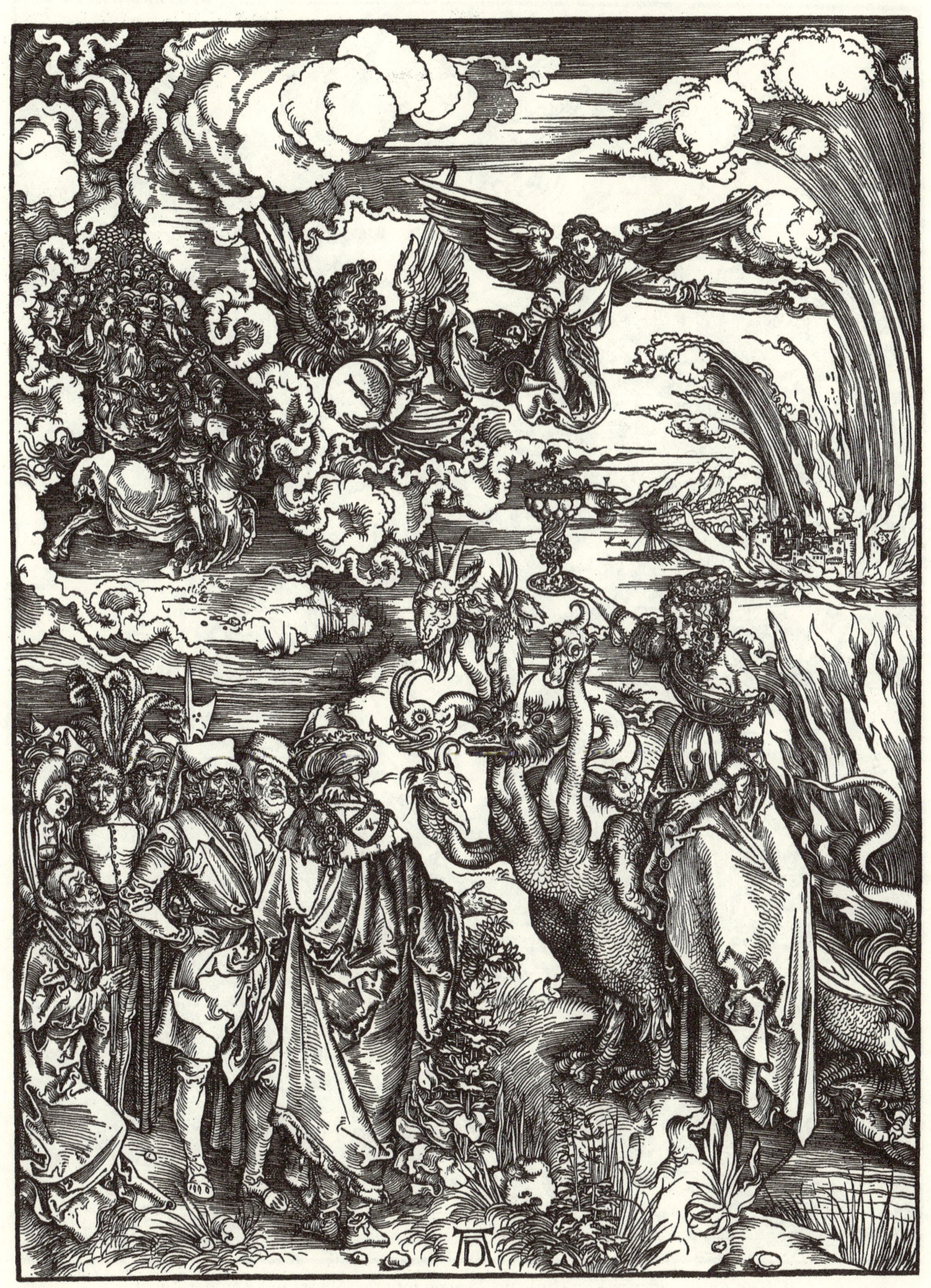

20. The Whore of Babylon

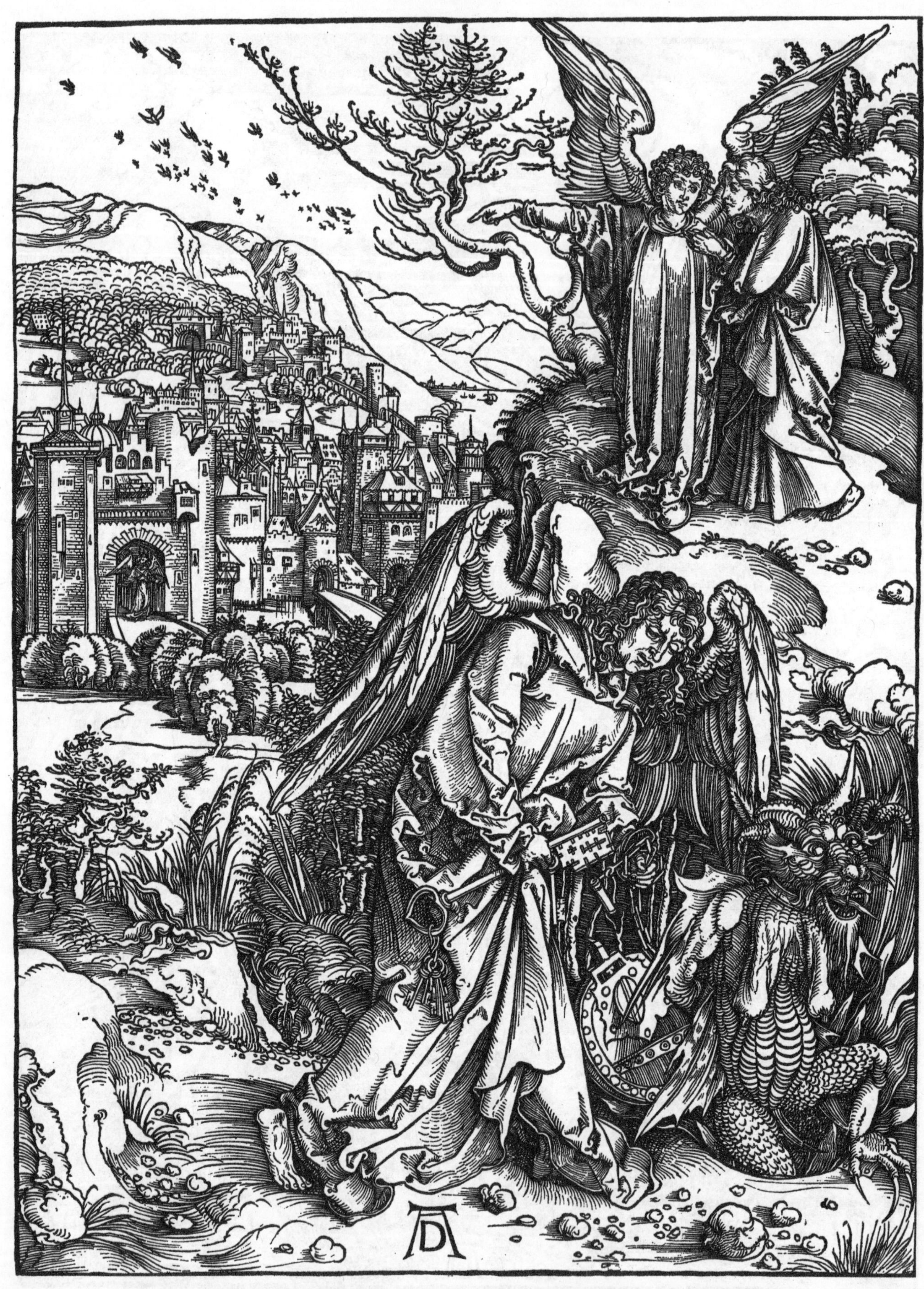

21. The Angel with the Key Hurls the Dragon into the Abyss, and Another Angel Shows S. John the New Jerusalem

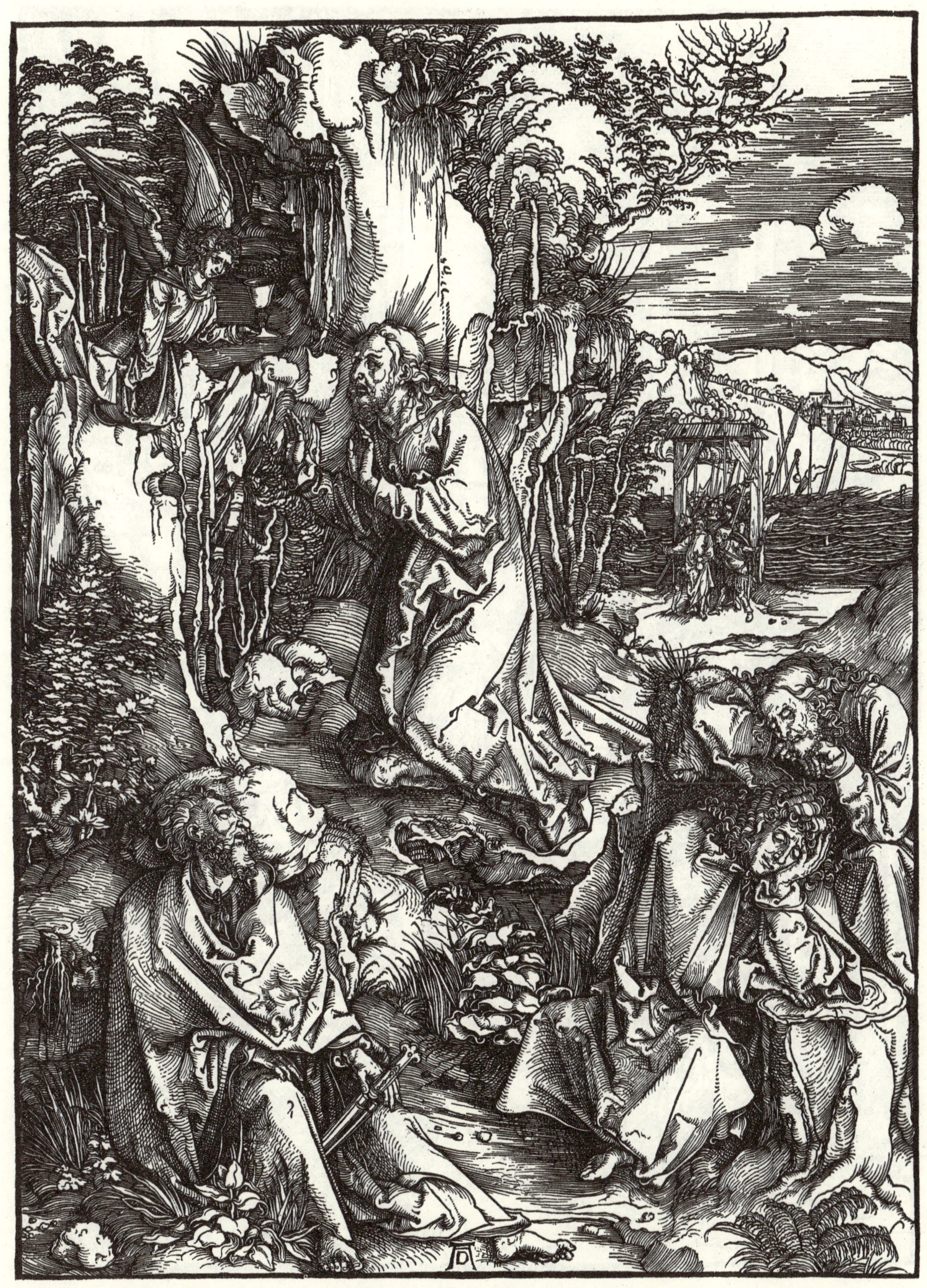

22. Christ on the Mount of Olives

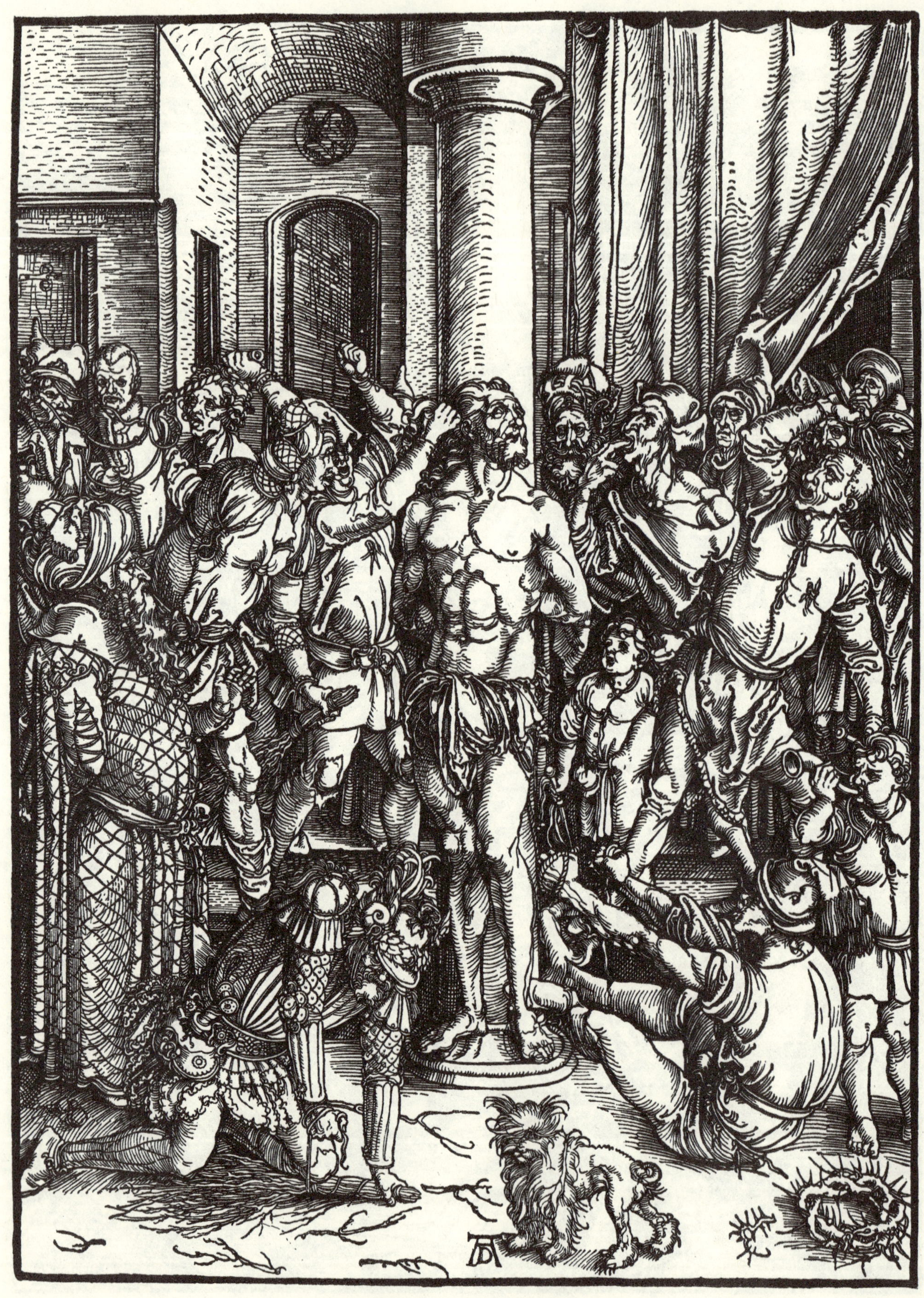

23. The Flagellation of Christ

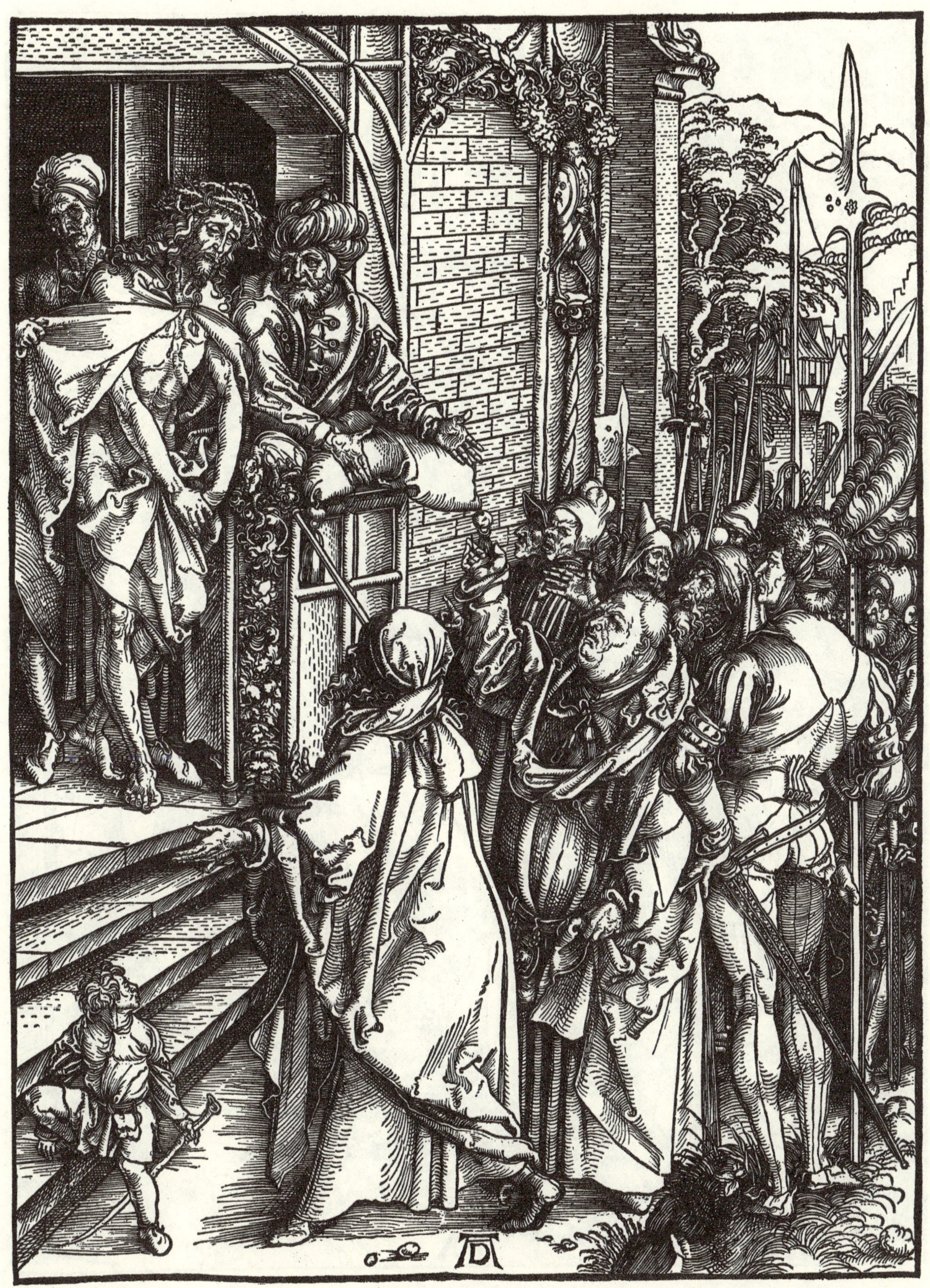

24. Christ Before the People

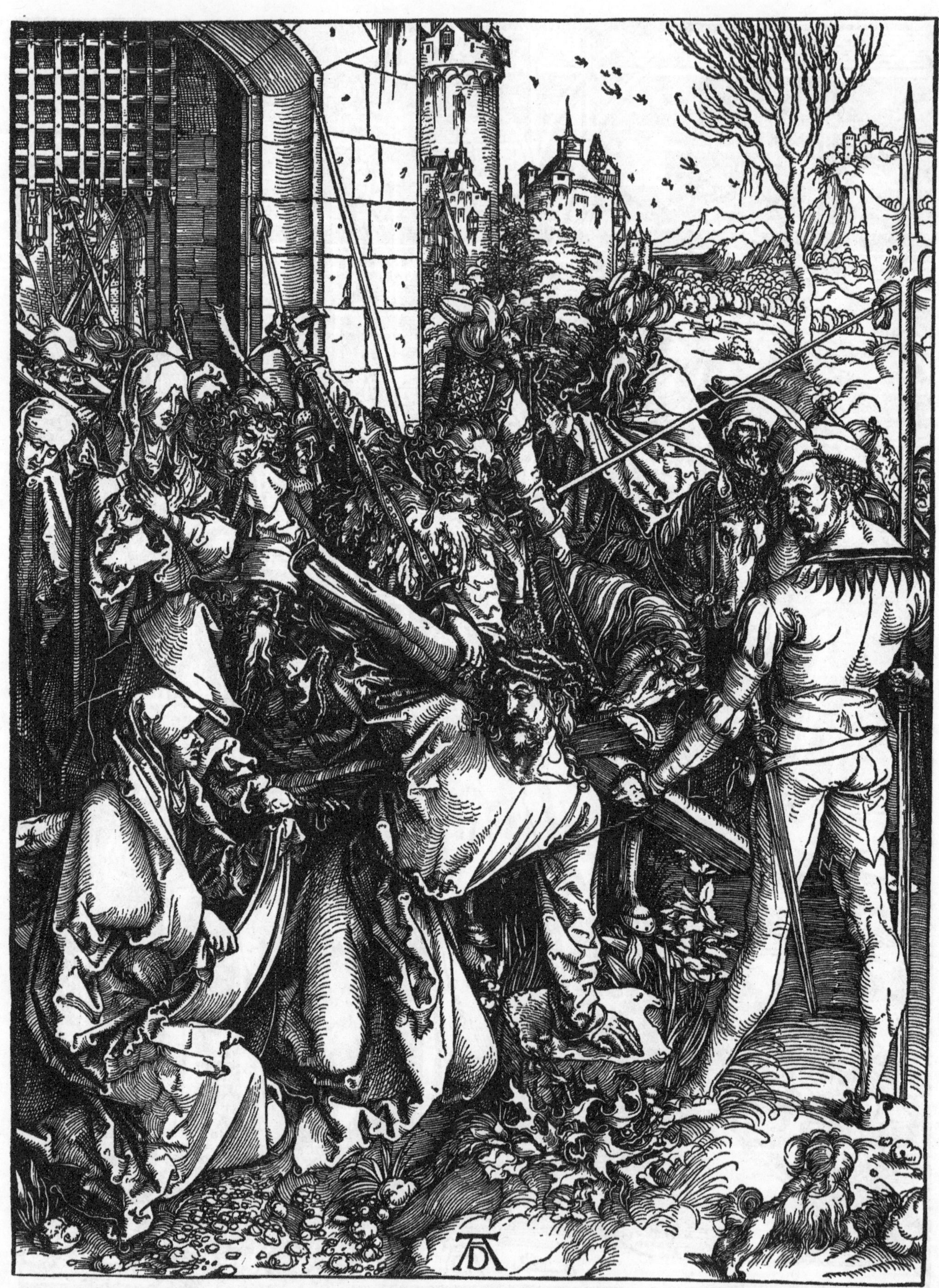

25. Christ Bearing the Cross

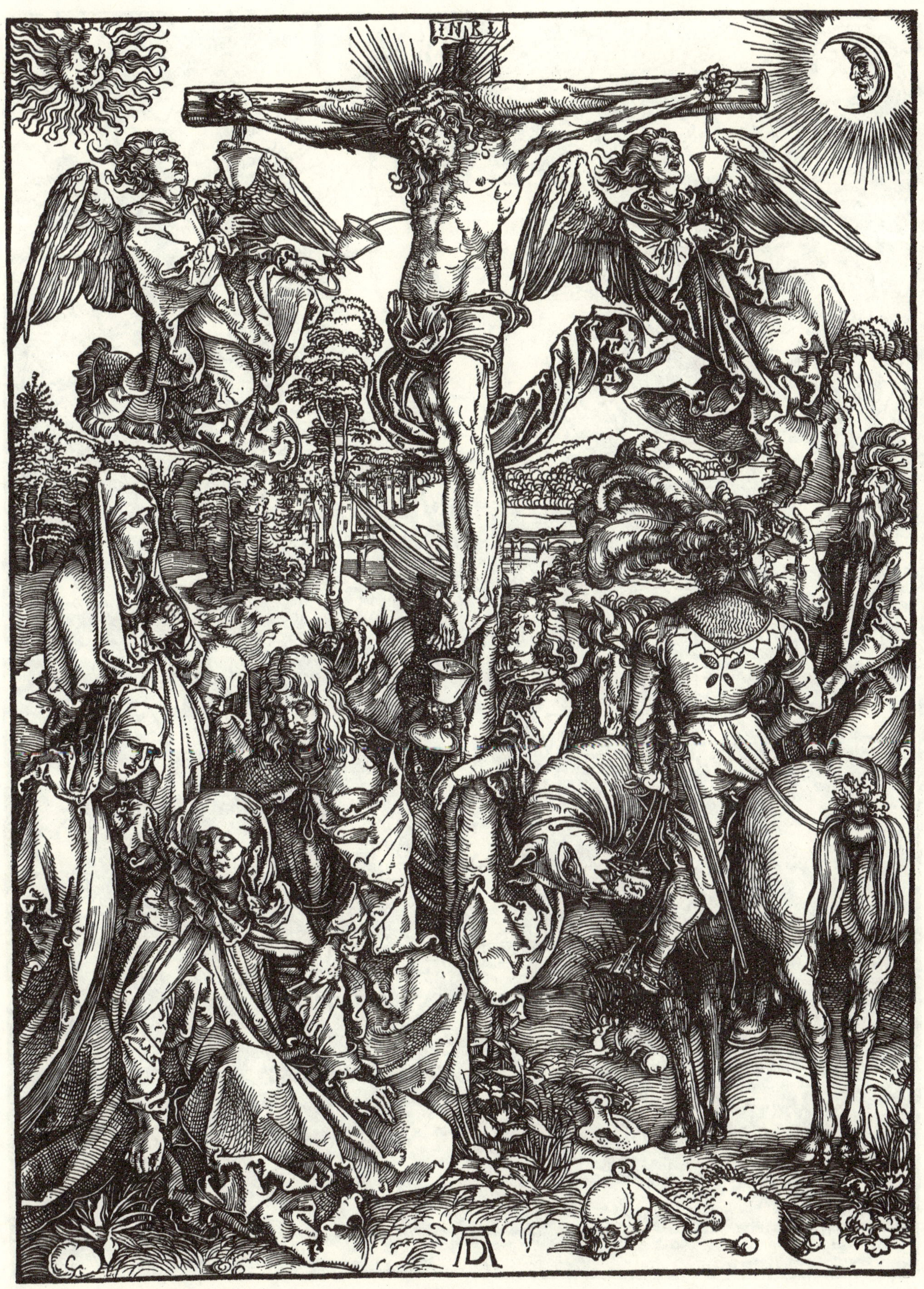

26. The Crucifixion

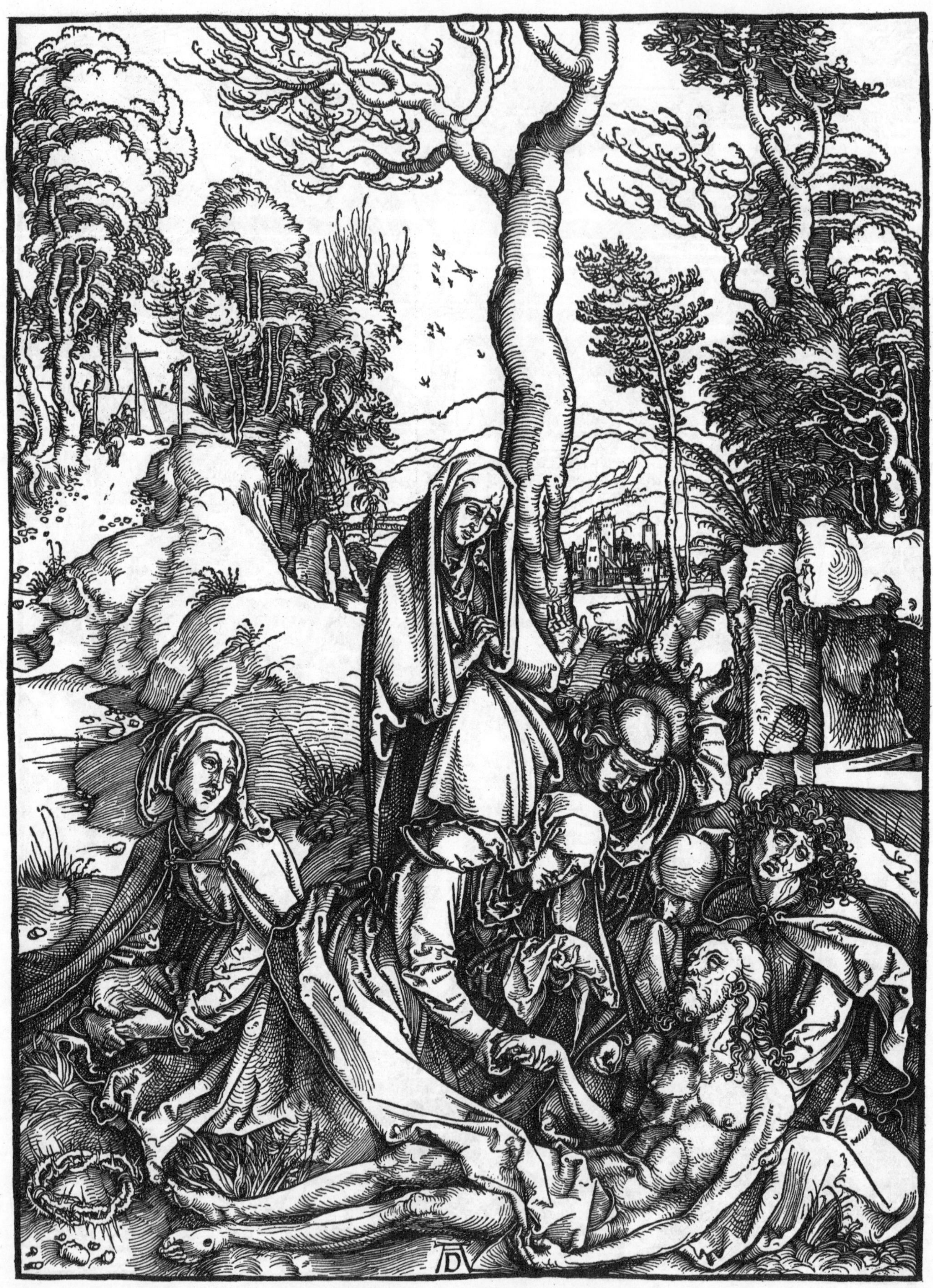

27. The Lamentation for Christ

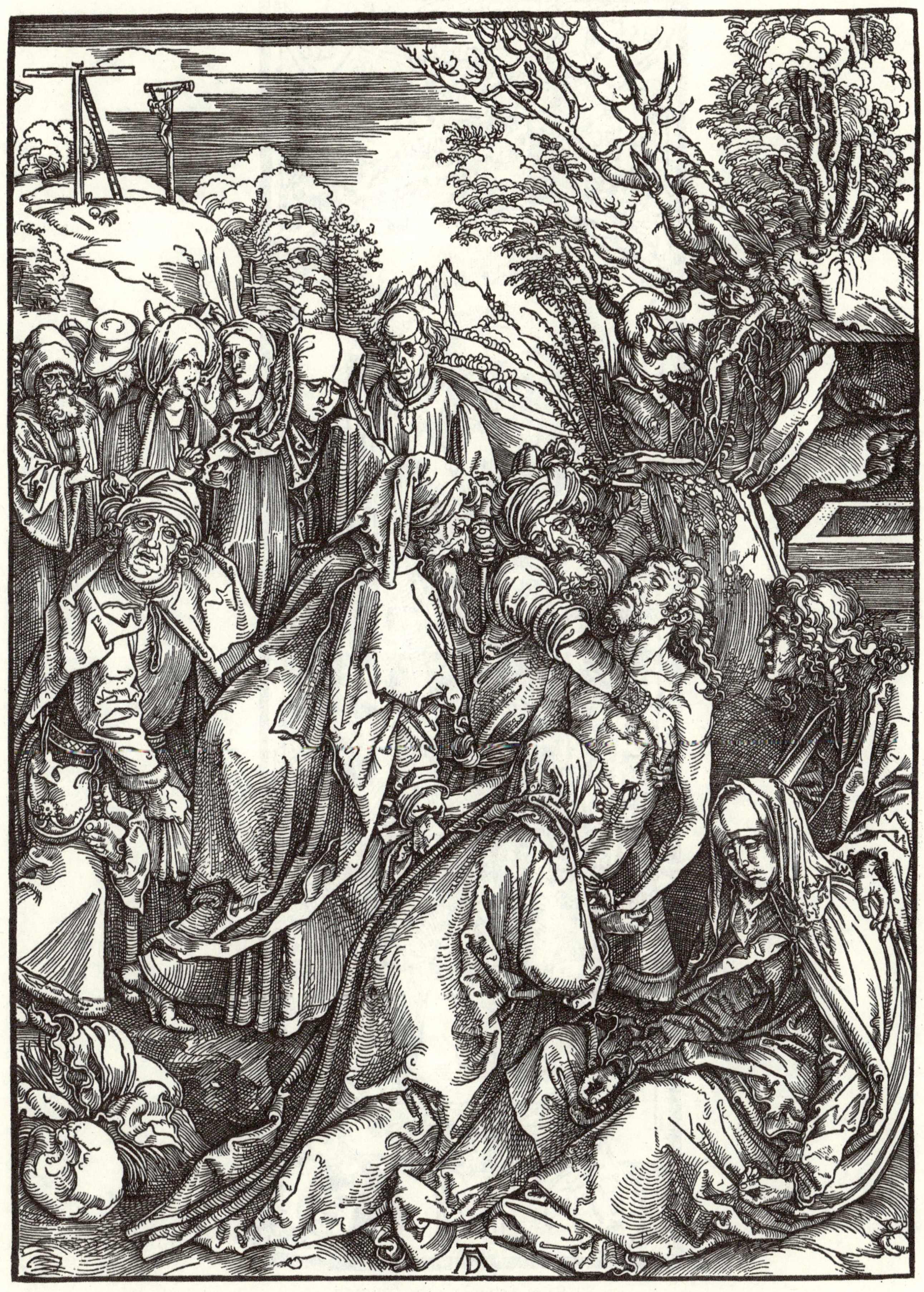

28. The Entombment

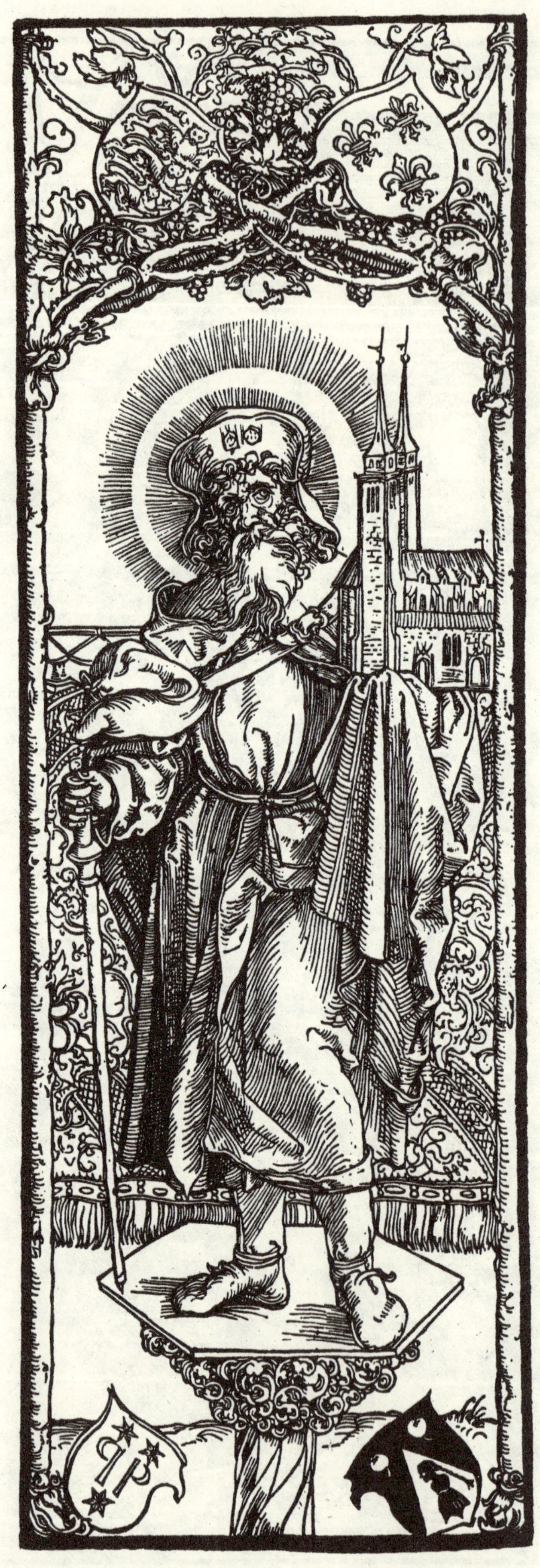

29. Saint Sebald on the Column

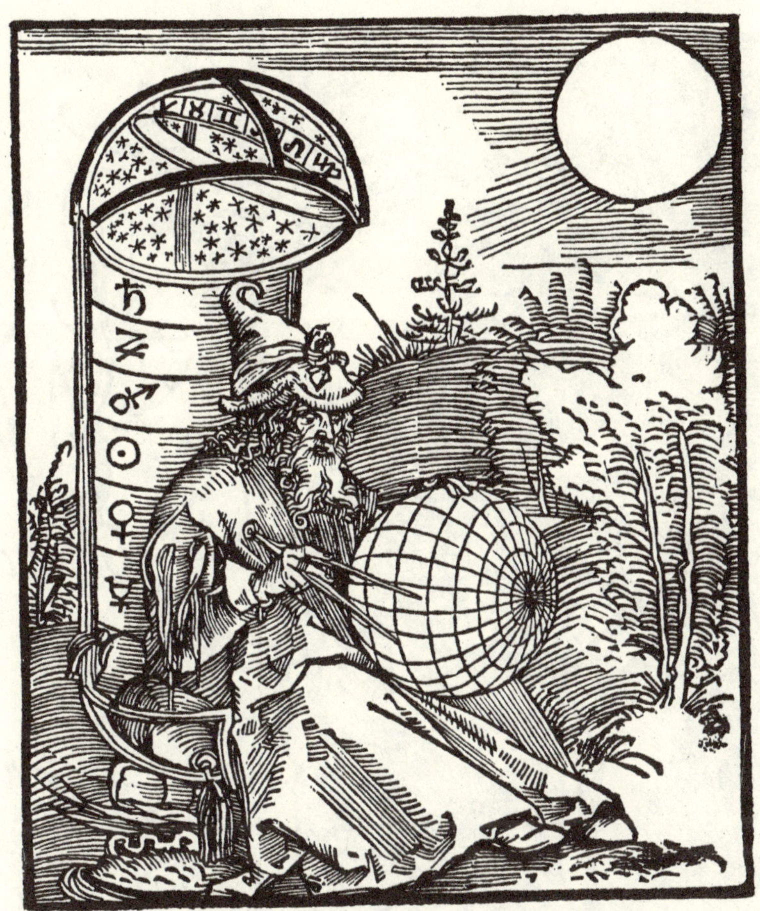

30. Astronomer

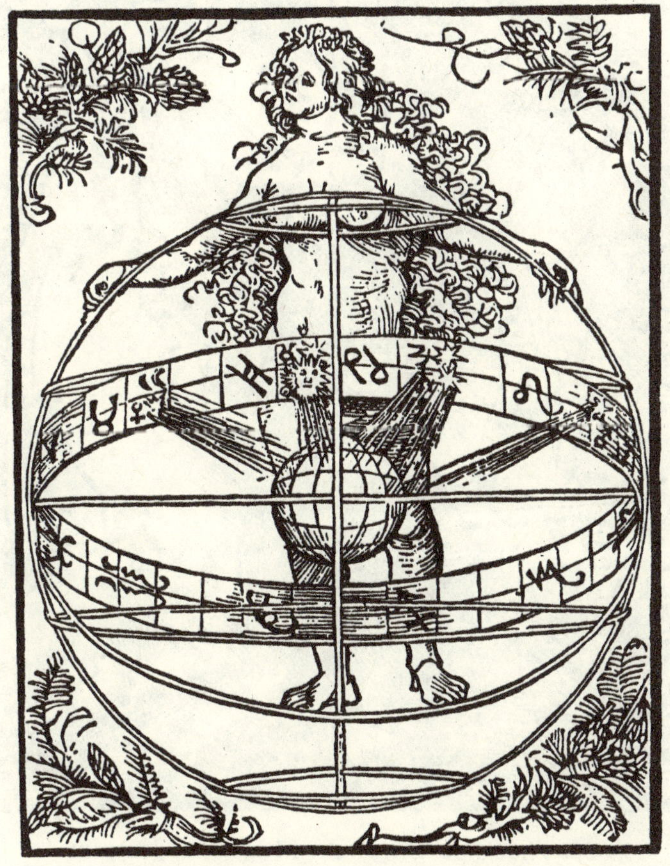

31. Nude Woman with the Zodiac

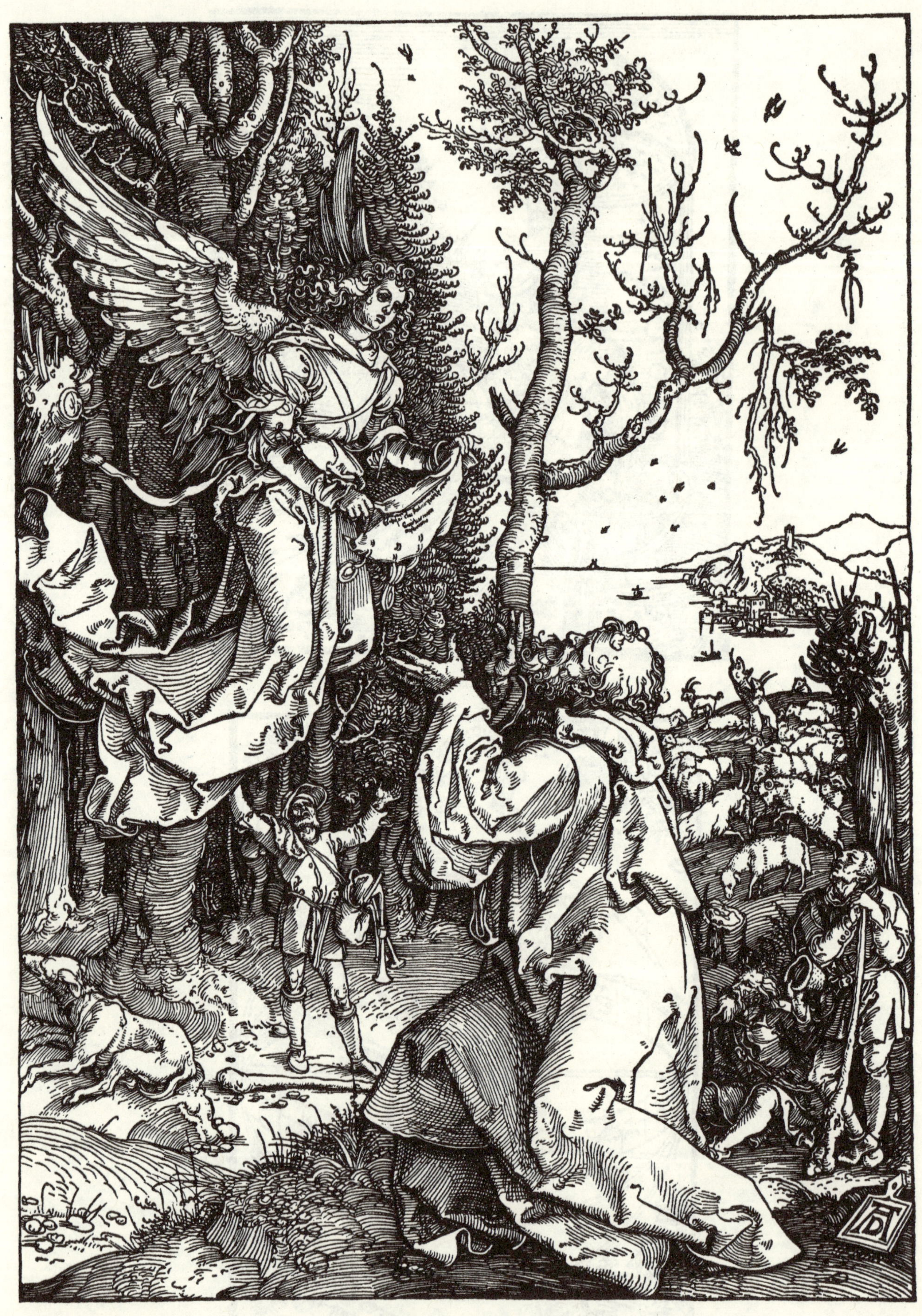

32. The Angel Brings the Message to Joachim

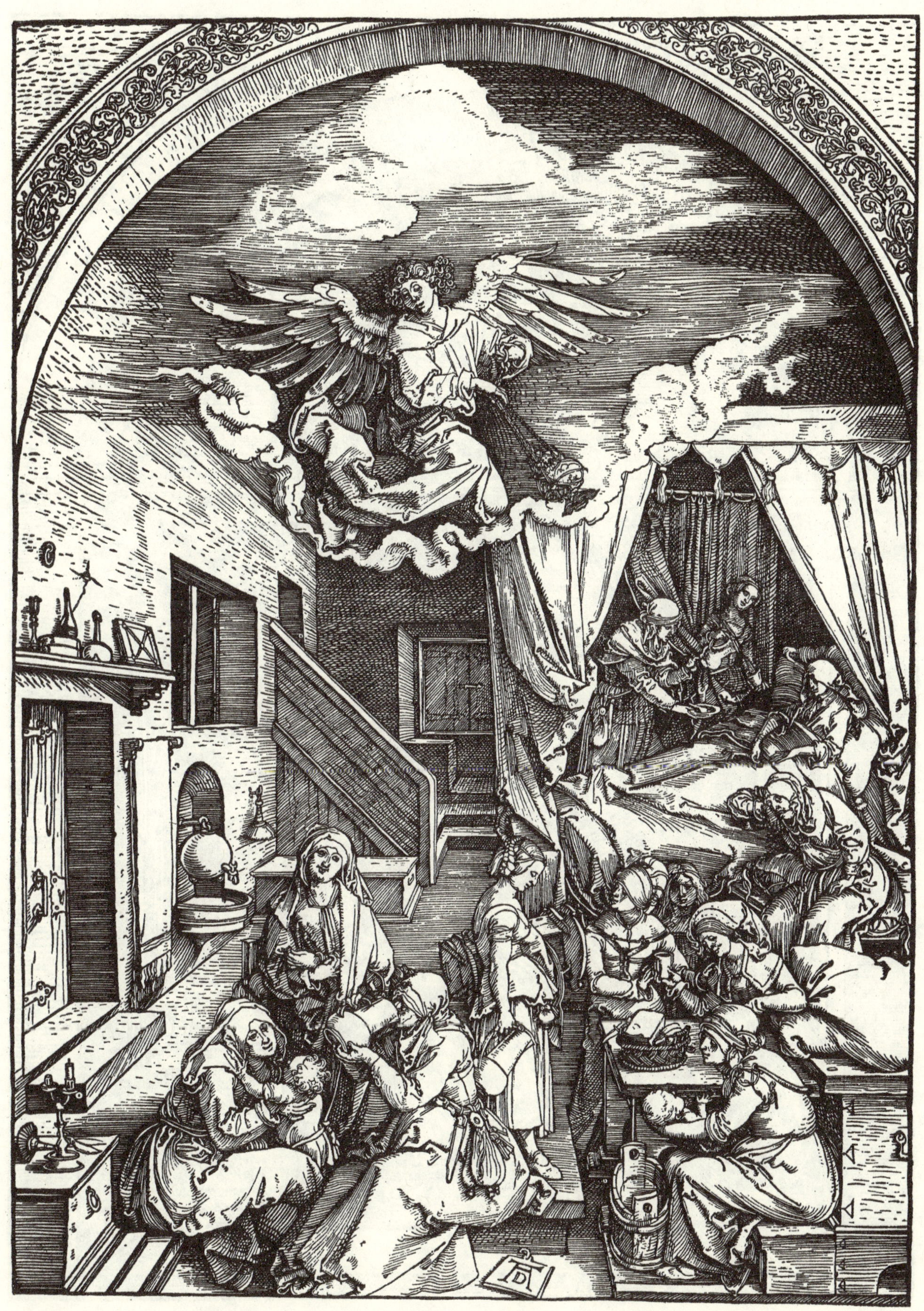

33. The Birth of Mary

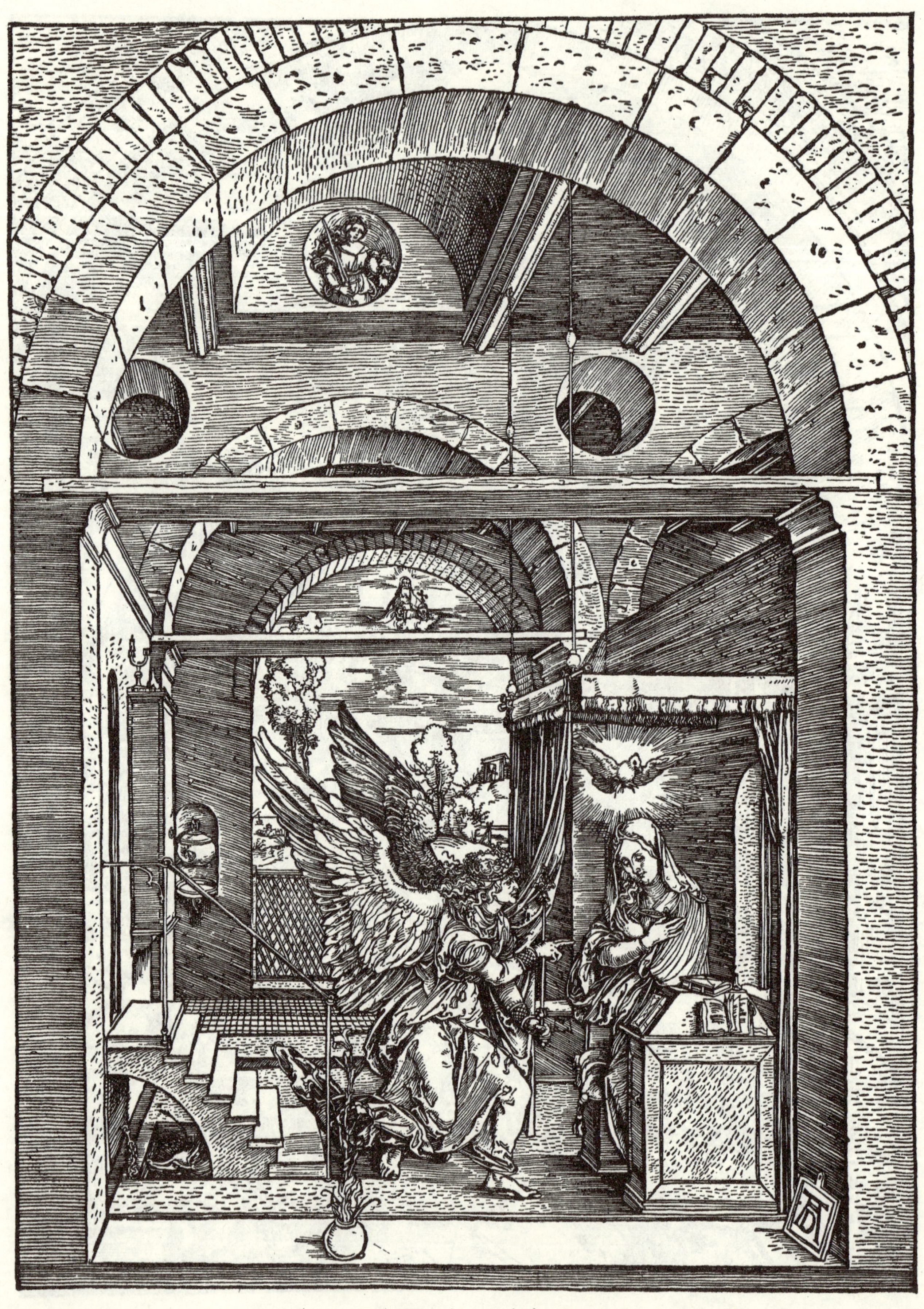

34. The Annunciation

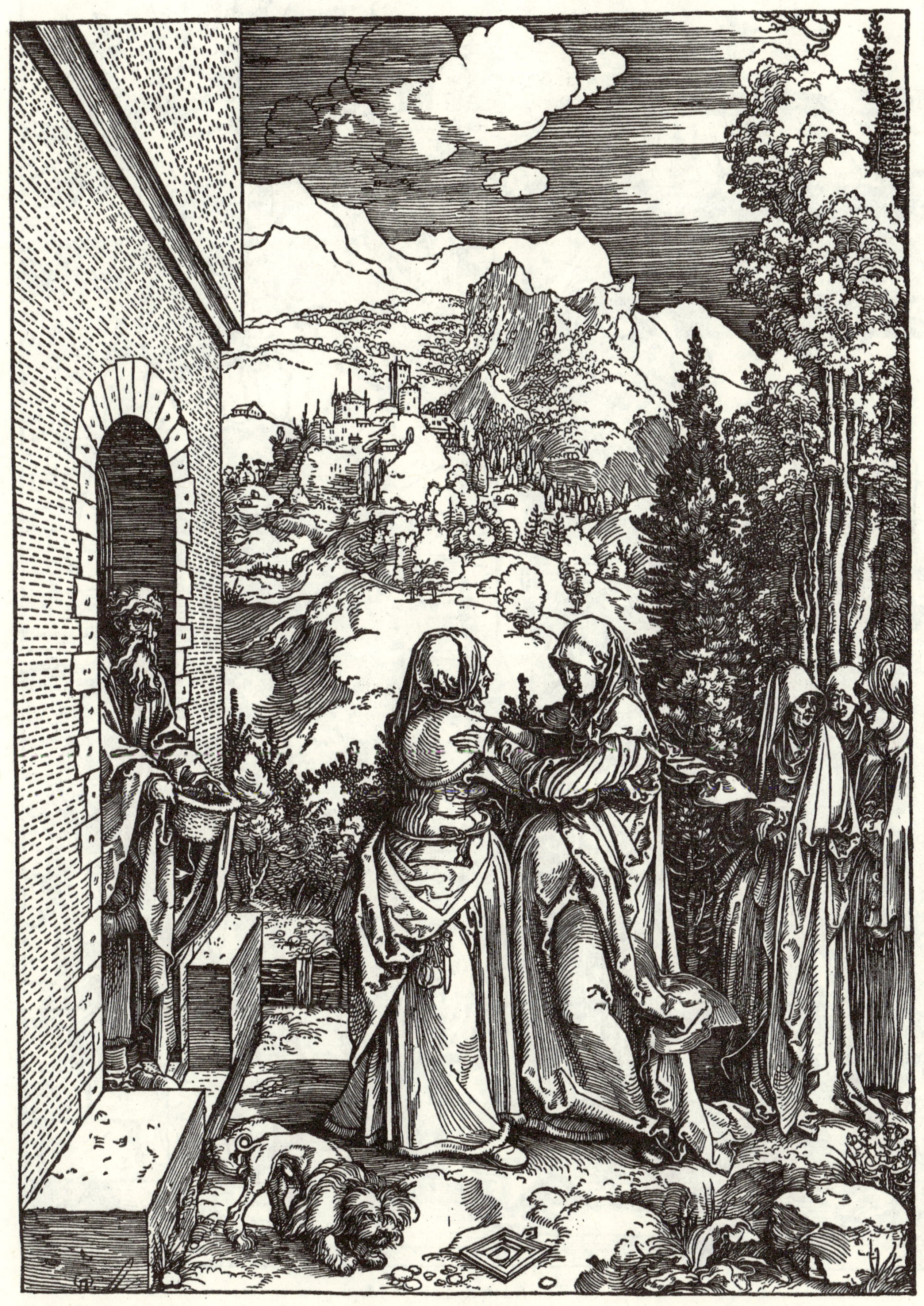

35. The Visitation

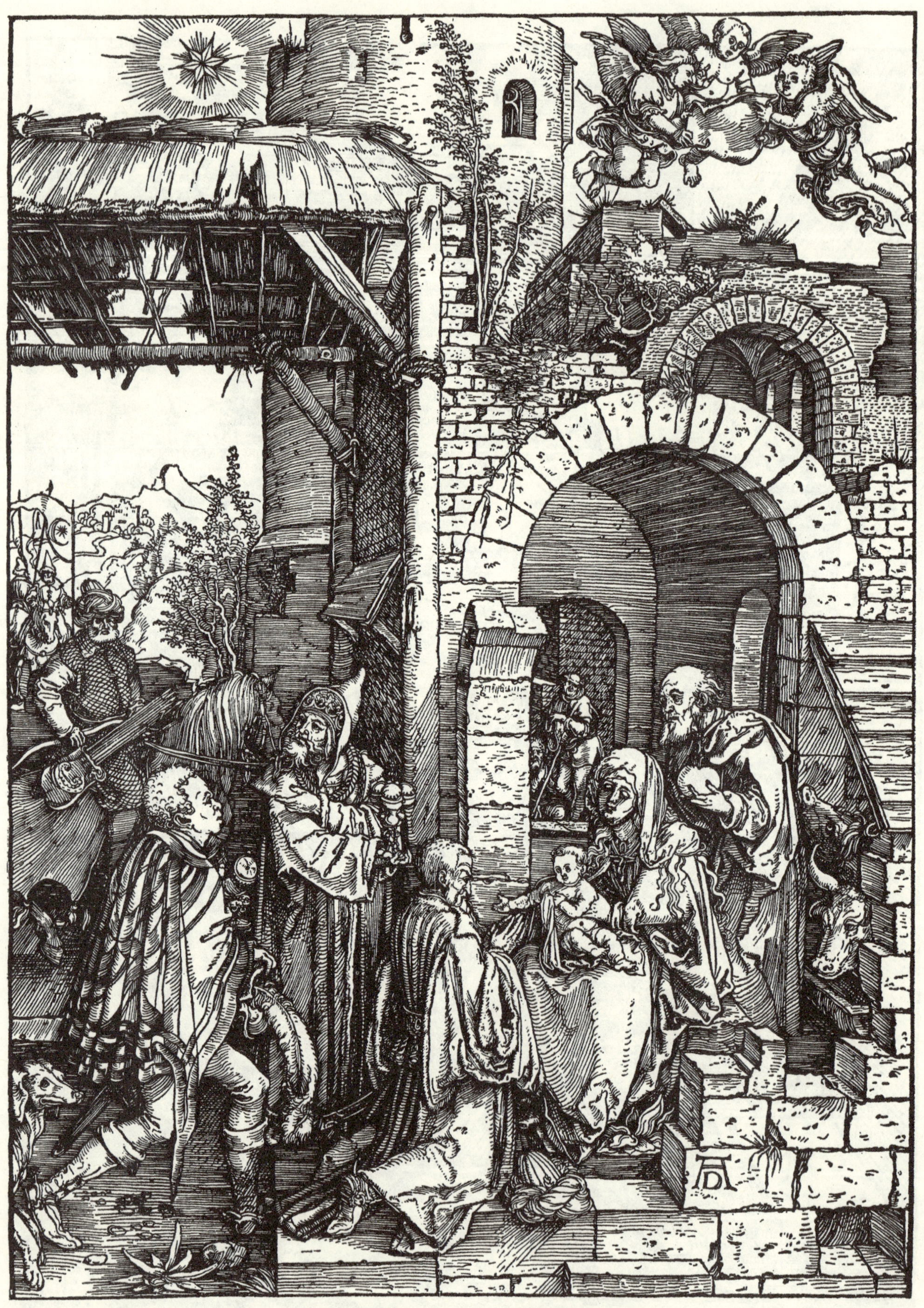

36. The Adoration of the Magi

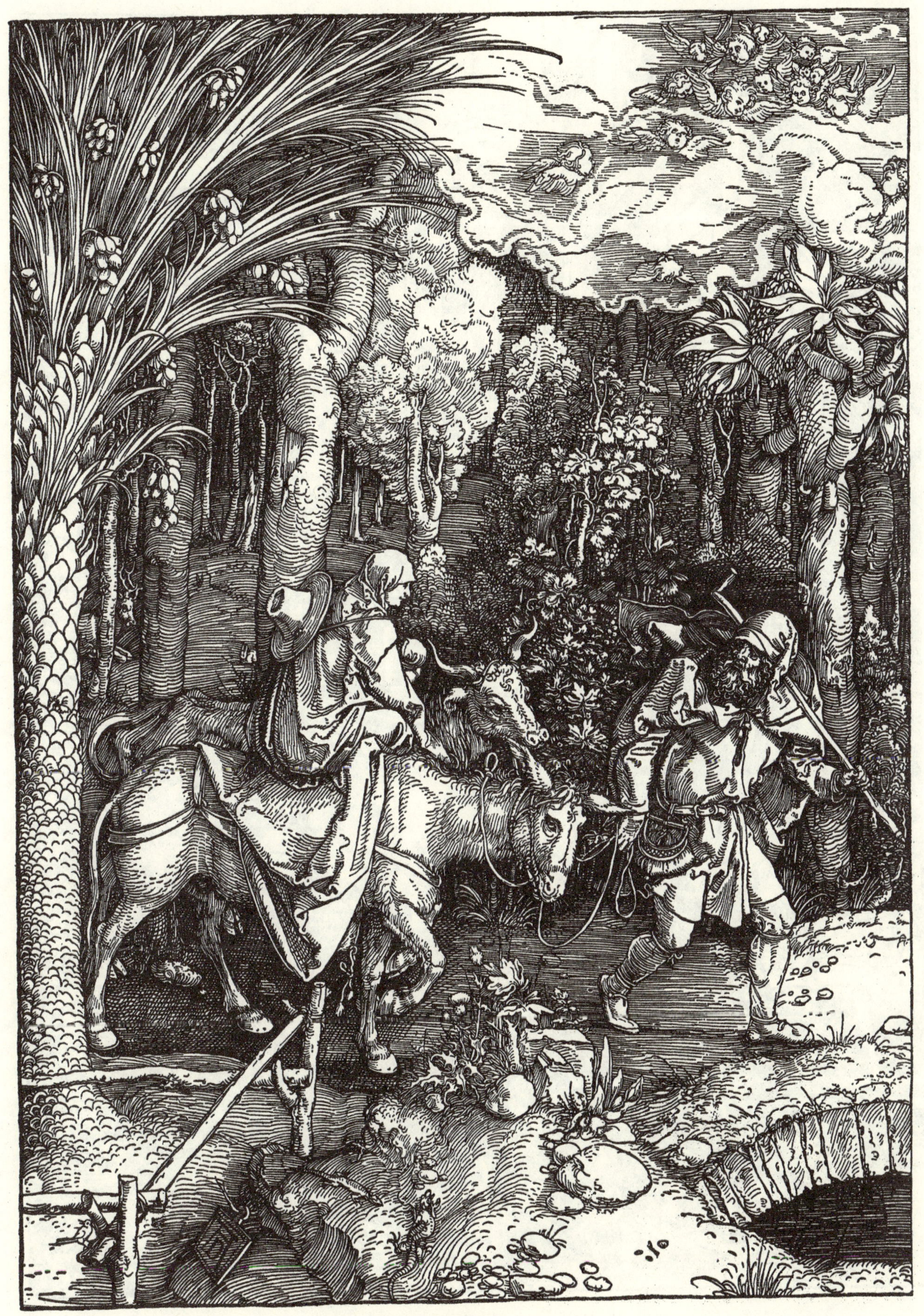

37. The Flight into Egypt

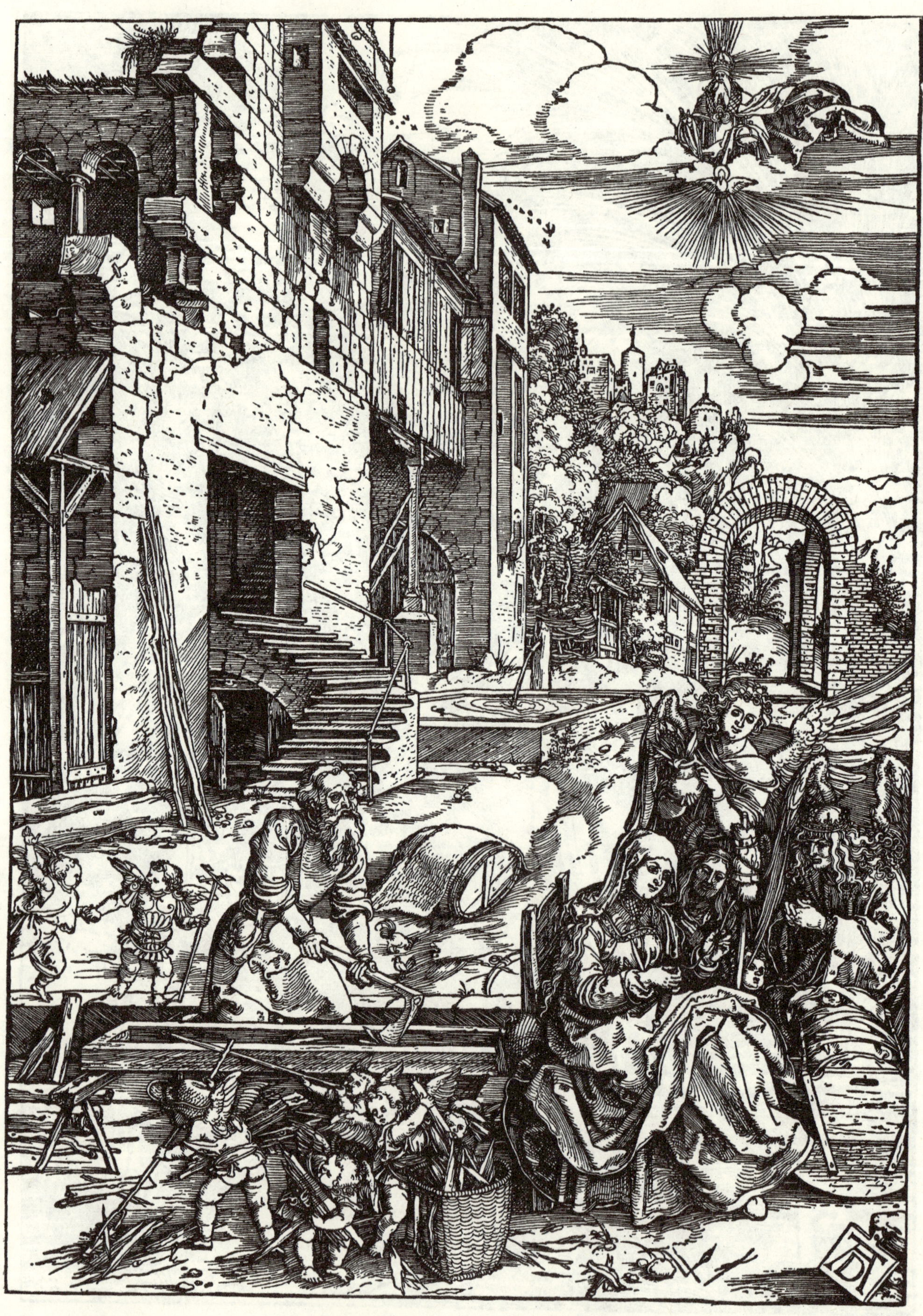

38. Repose on the Flight into Egypt

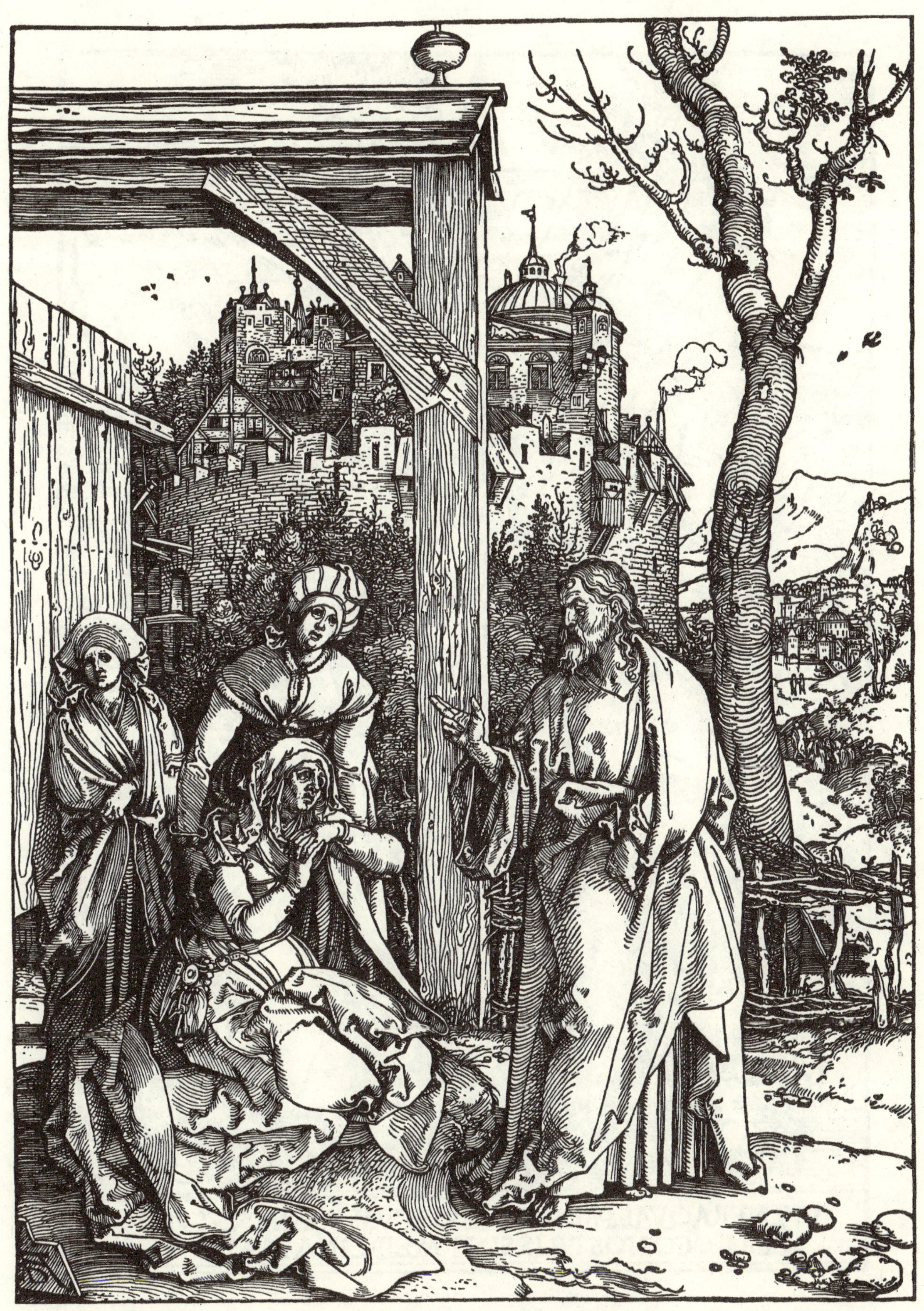

39. Christ Taking Leave of His Mother

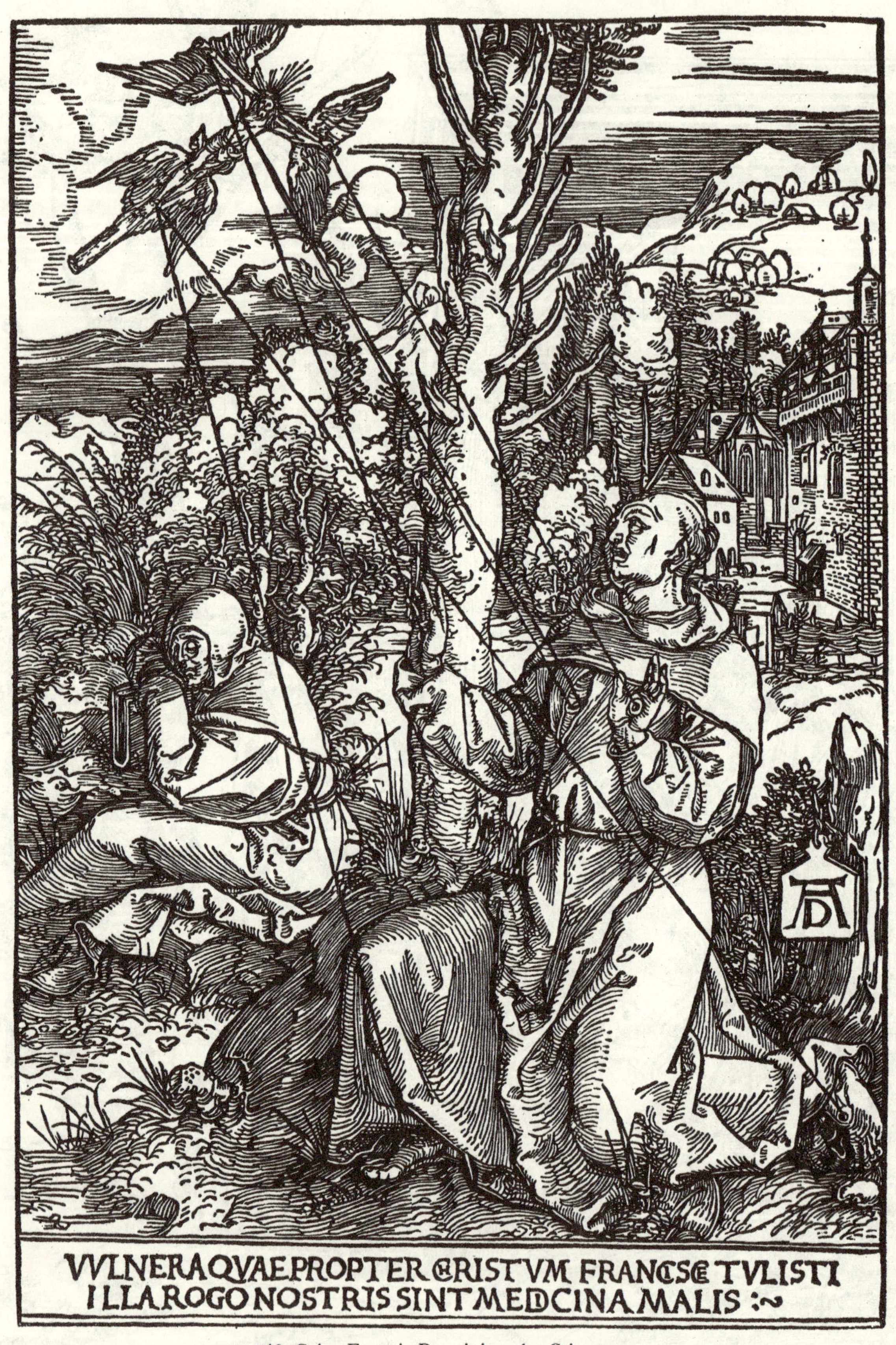

40. Saint Francis Receiving the Stigmata

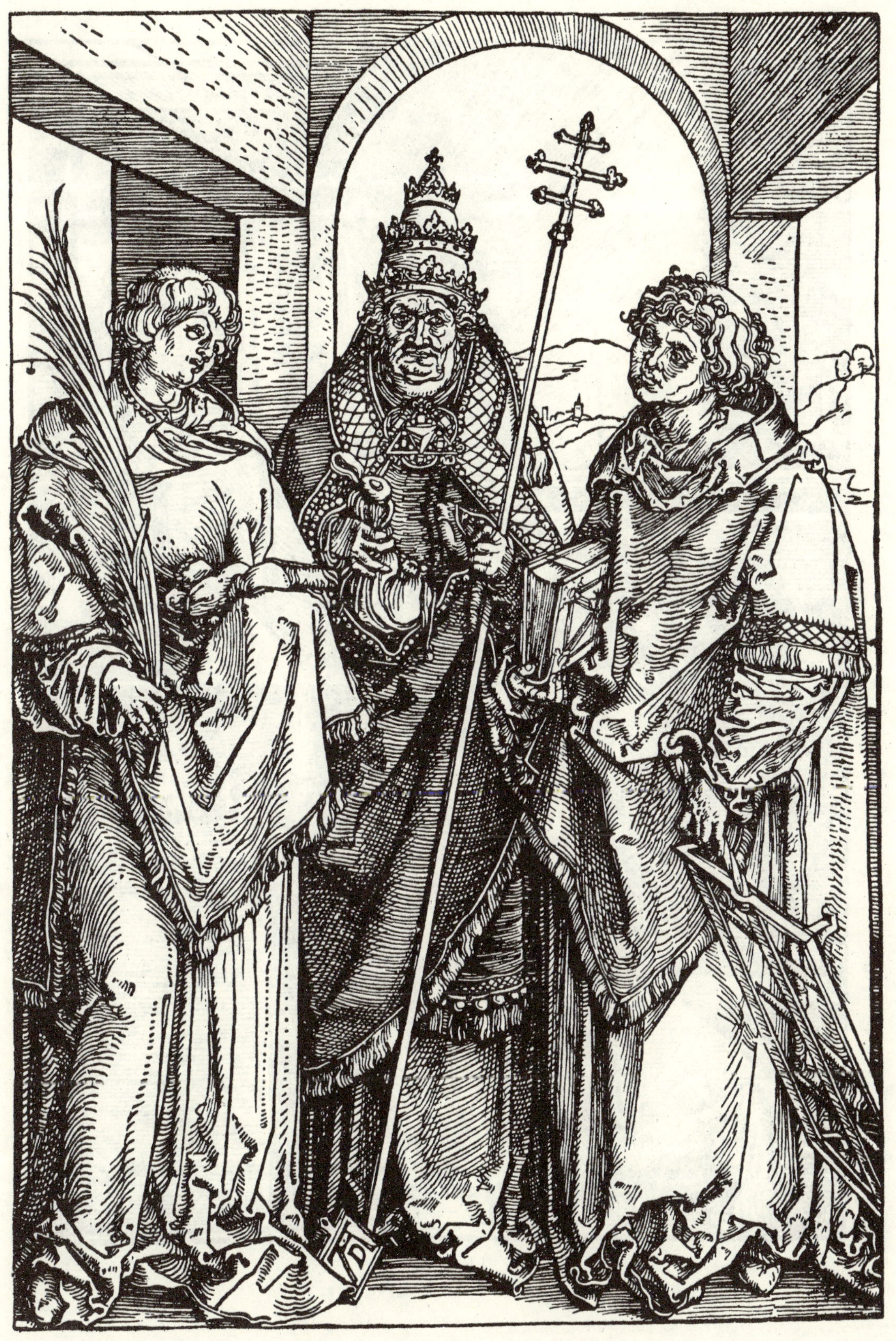

41. S. Stephen, S. Sixtus and S. Lawrence

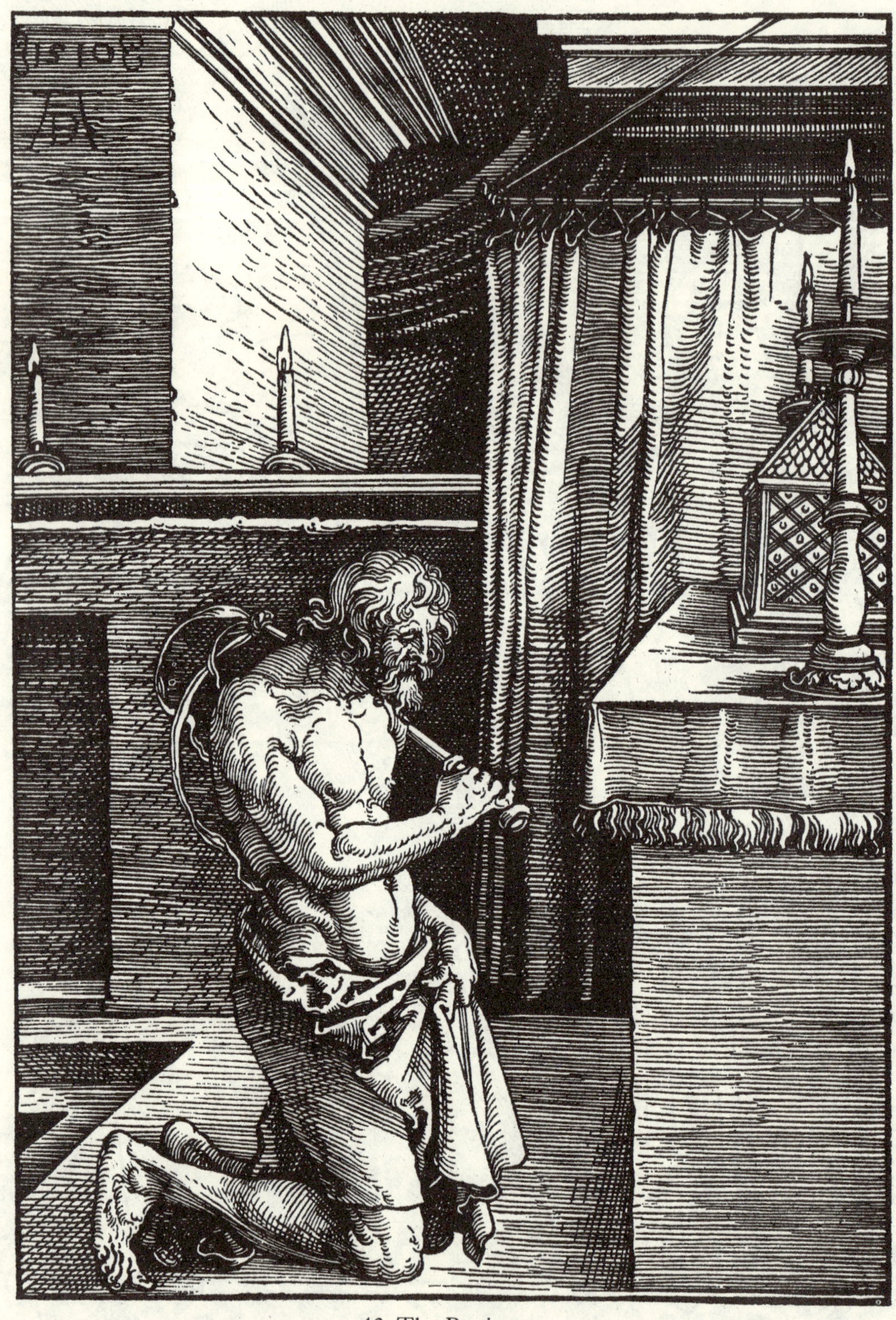

42. The Penitent

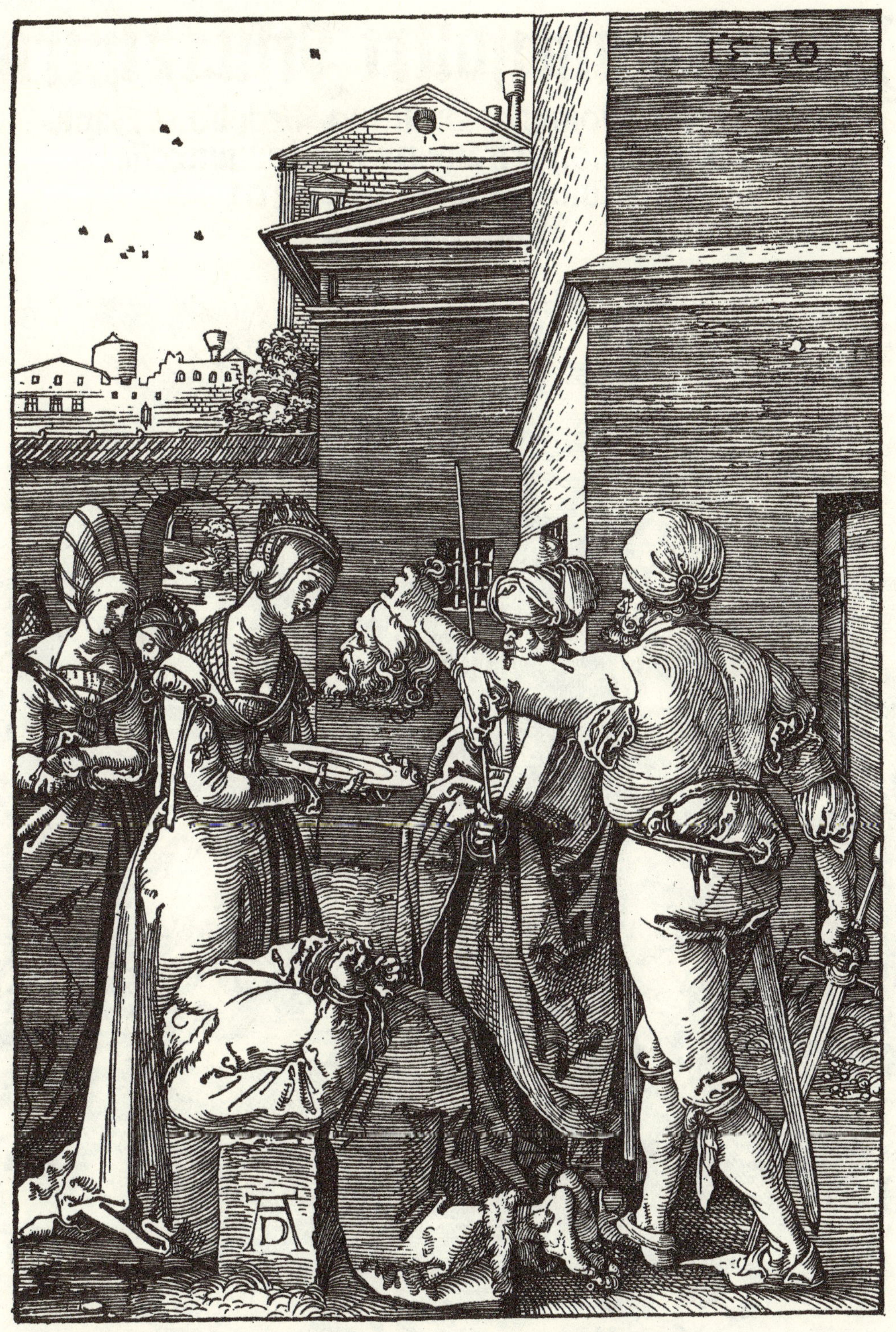

43. The Beheading of St. John the Baptist

Passio domini nostri Jesu. ex hierony
mo Paduano. Dominico Mancino. Sedulio. et Bapti-
sta Mantuano. per fratrem Chelidonium colle
cta. cum figuris Alberti Dureri
Norici Pictoris.

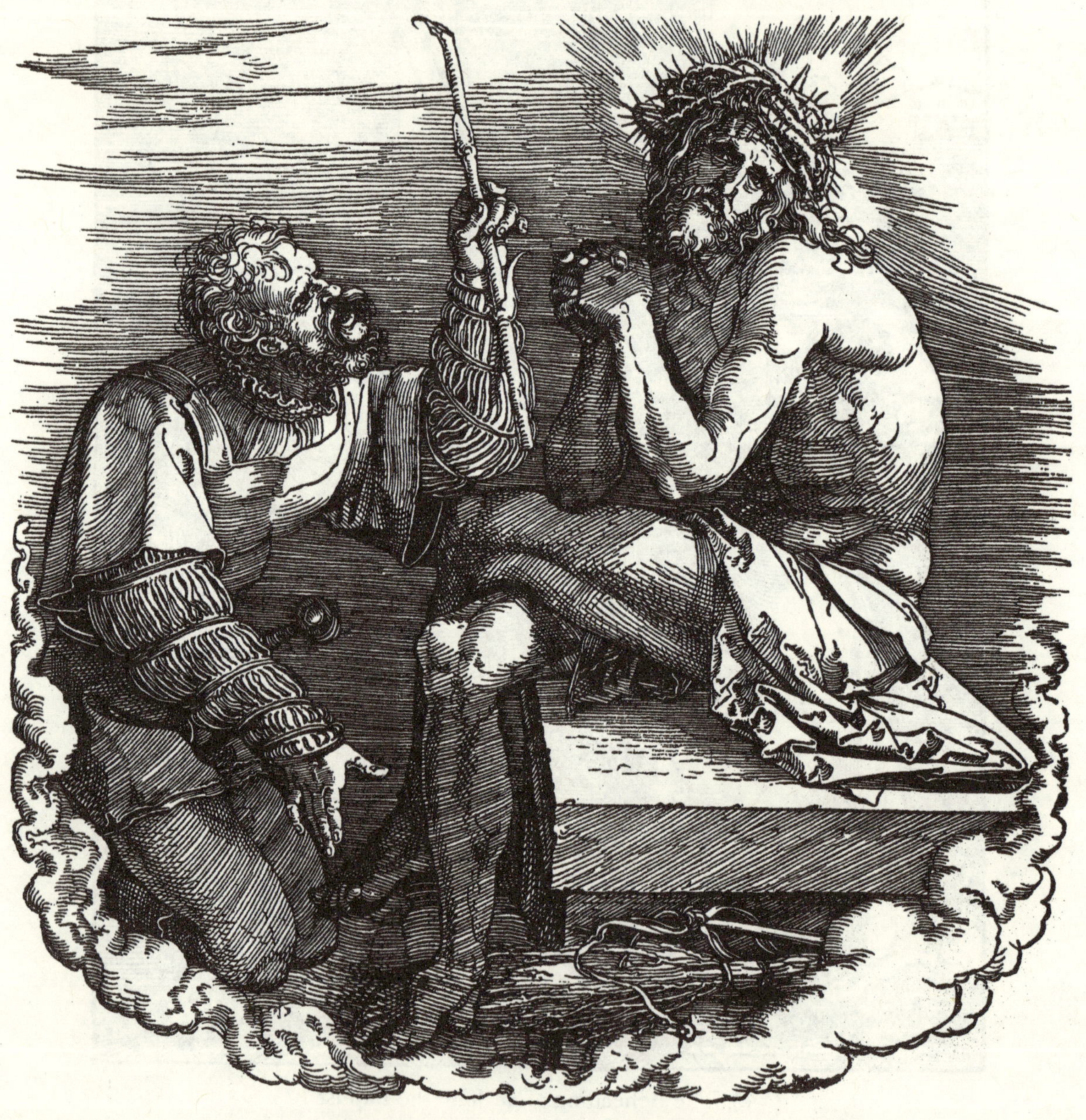

44. Title Page: The Mocking of Christ

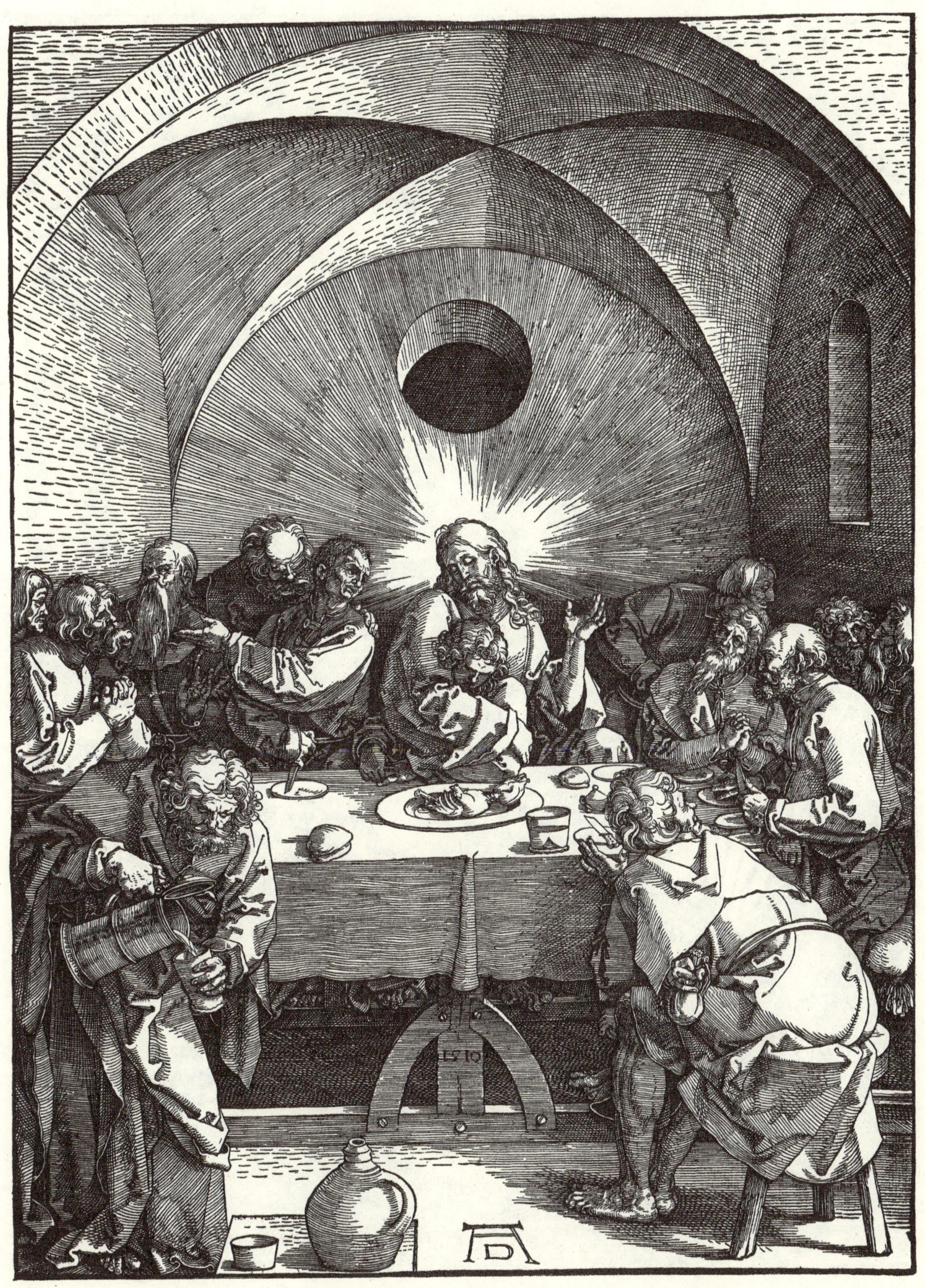

45. The Last Supper

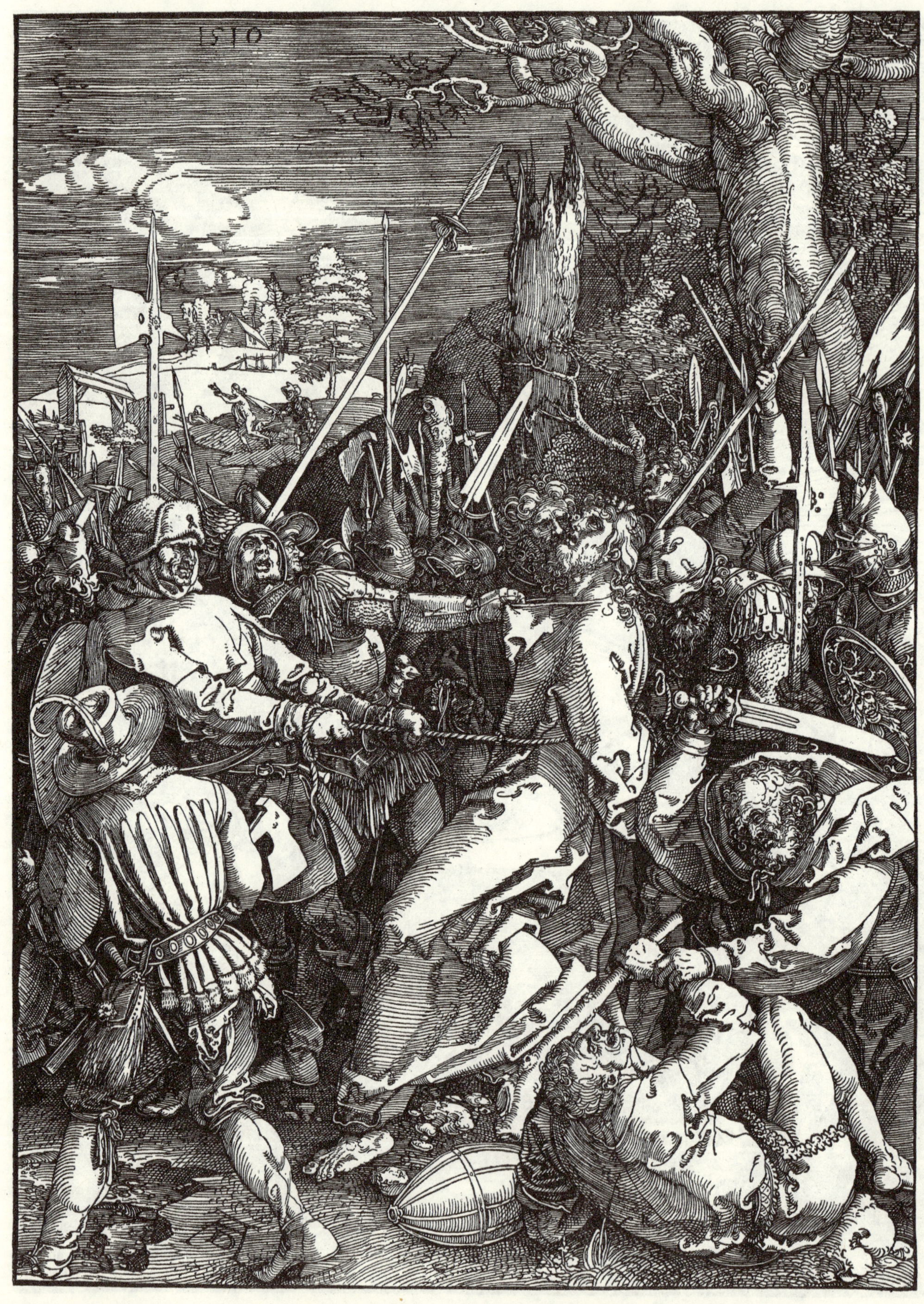

46. Christ Taken Captive

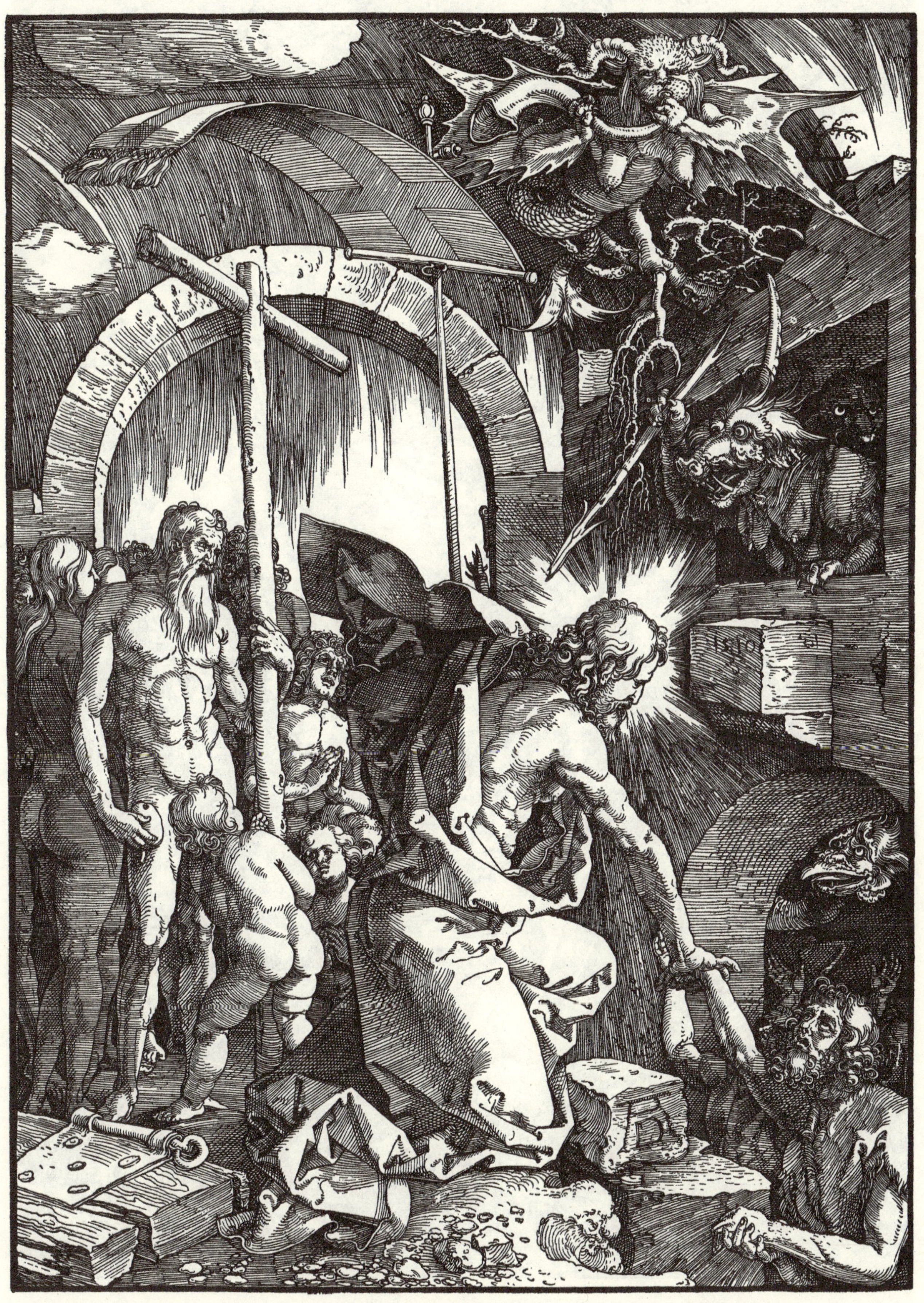

47. Christ in Limbo

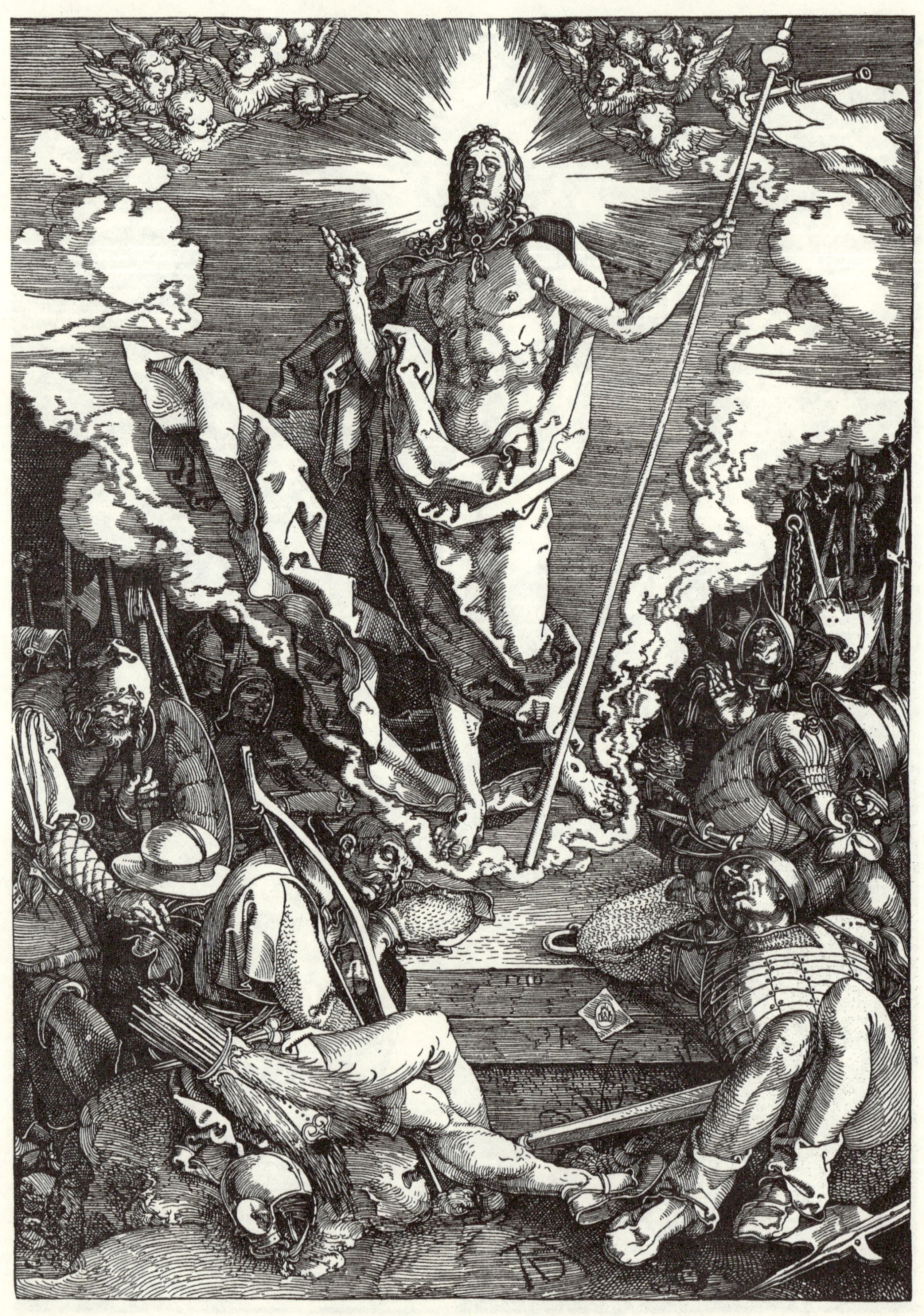

48. The Resurrection of Christ

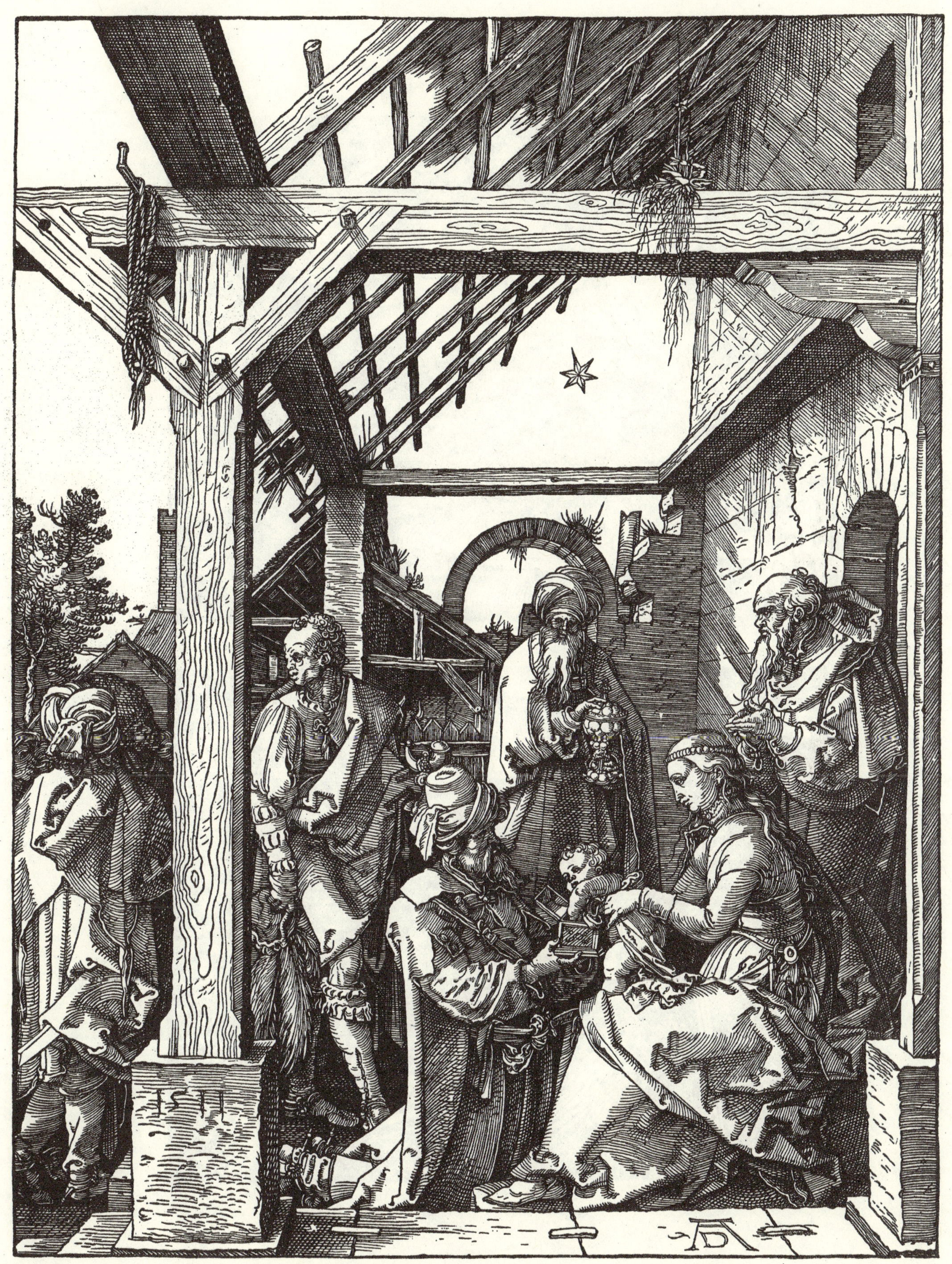

49. The Adoration of the Magi

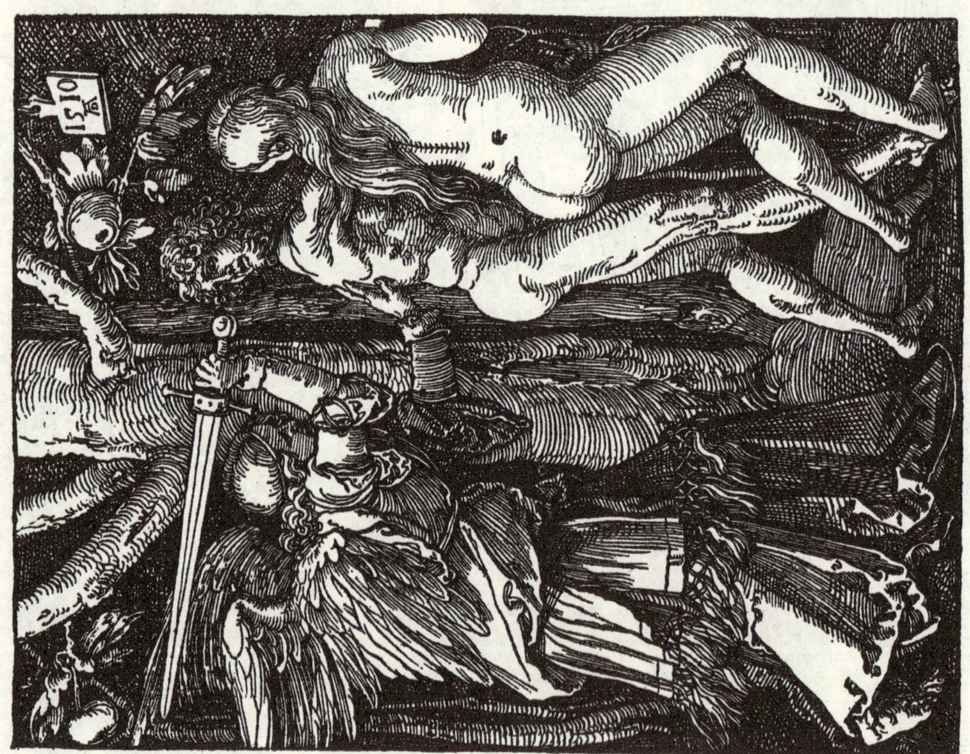

50. The Fall

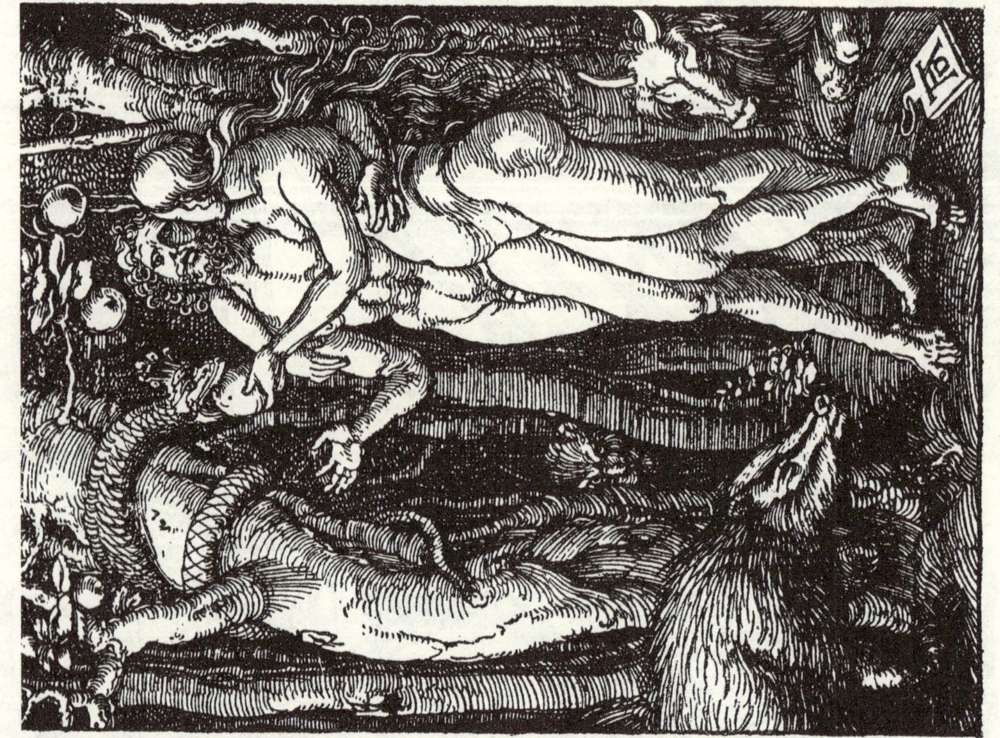

51. Expulsion from Paradise

52. The Head of St. John the Baptist Brought to Herod

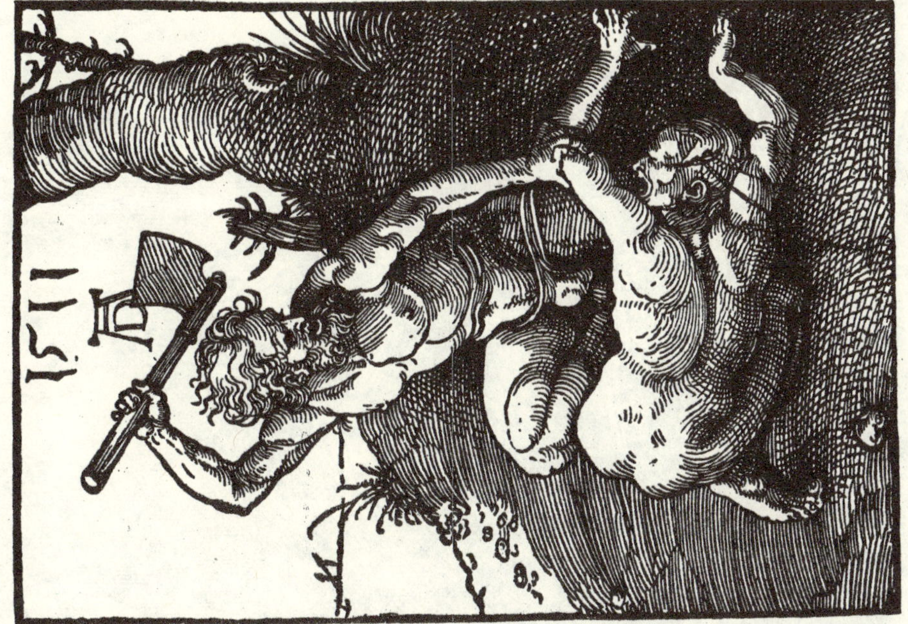

53. Cain Kills Abel

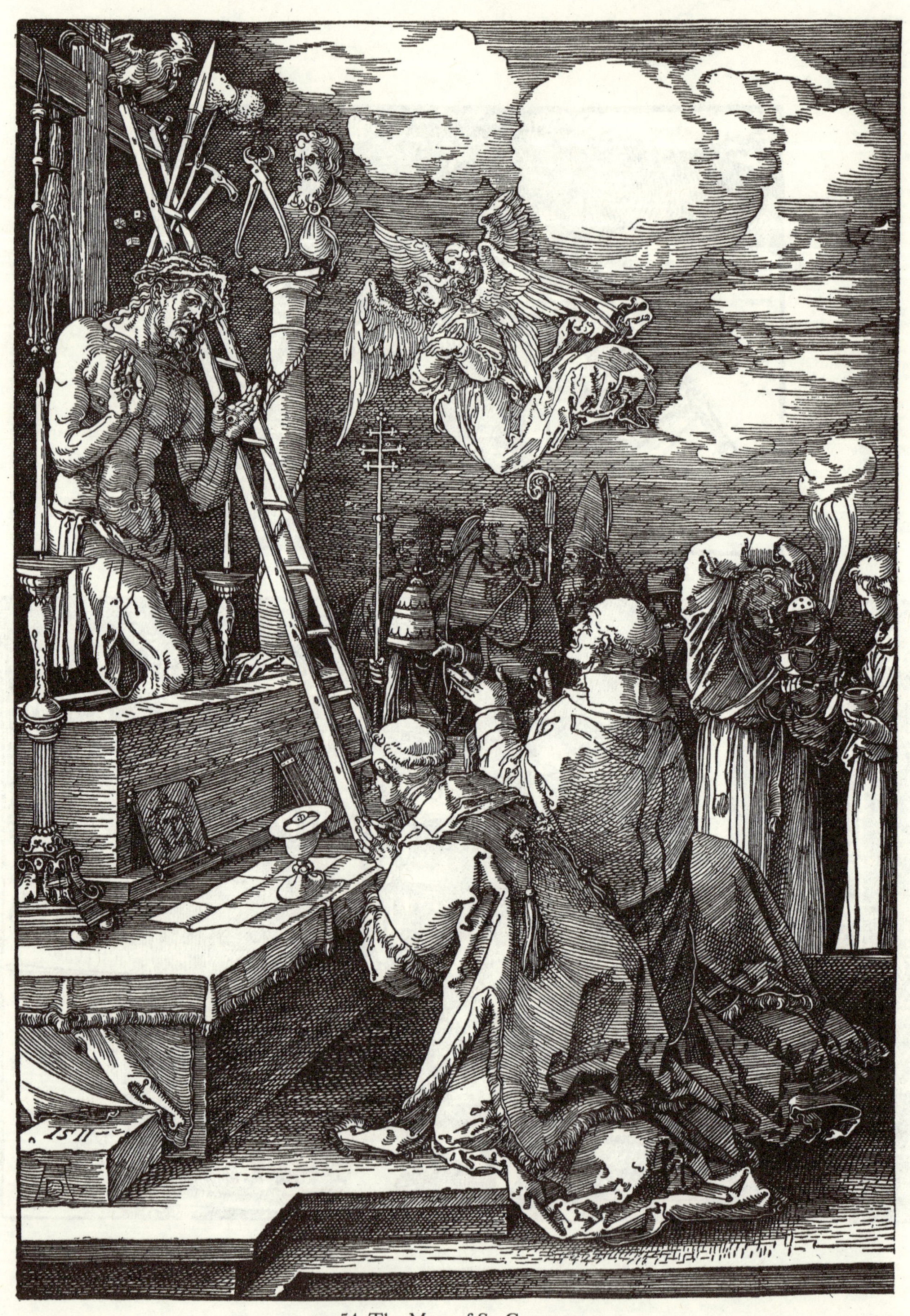

54. The Mass of St. Gregory

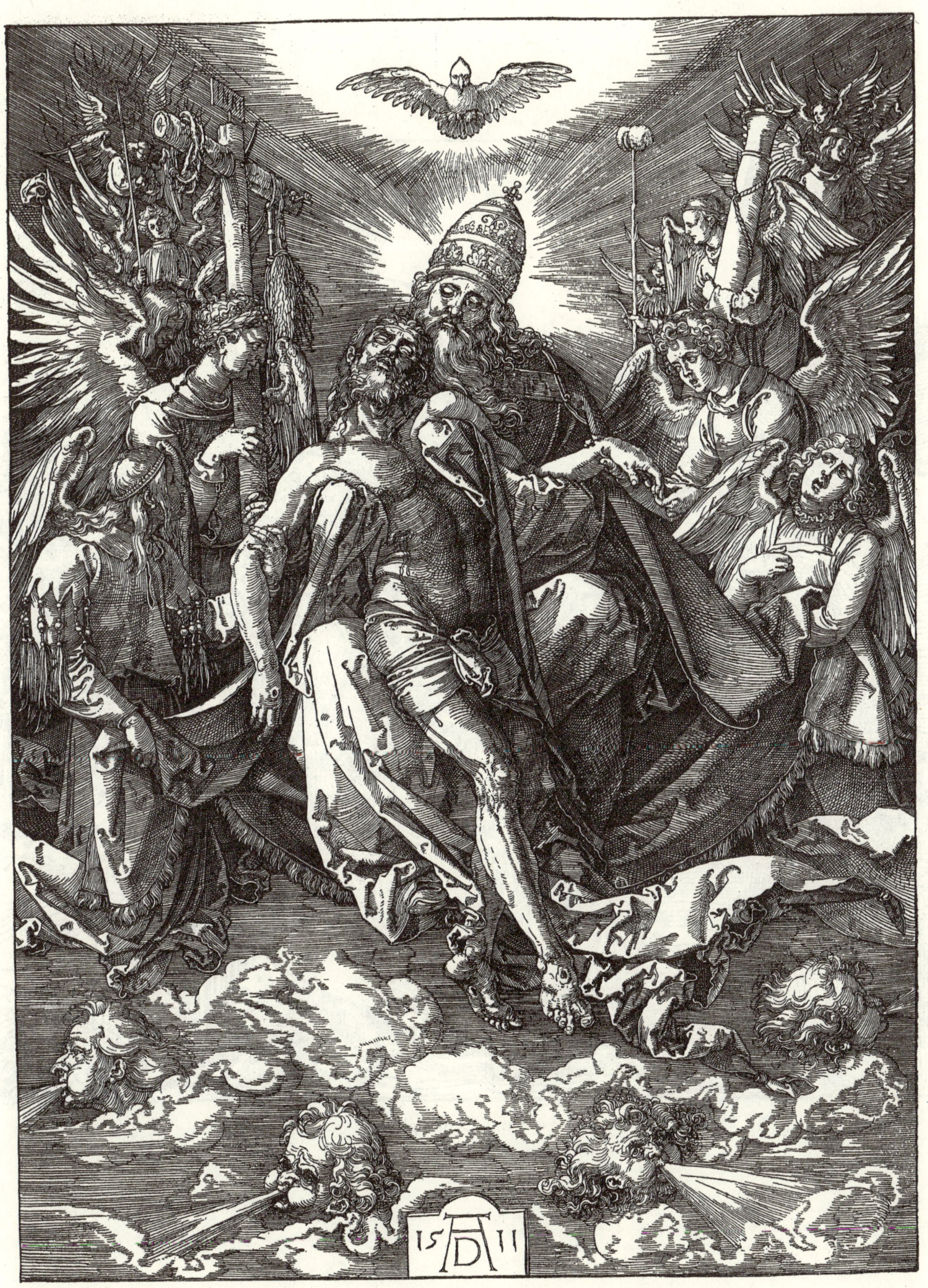

55. The Trinity

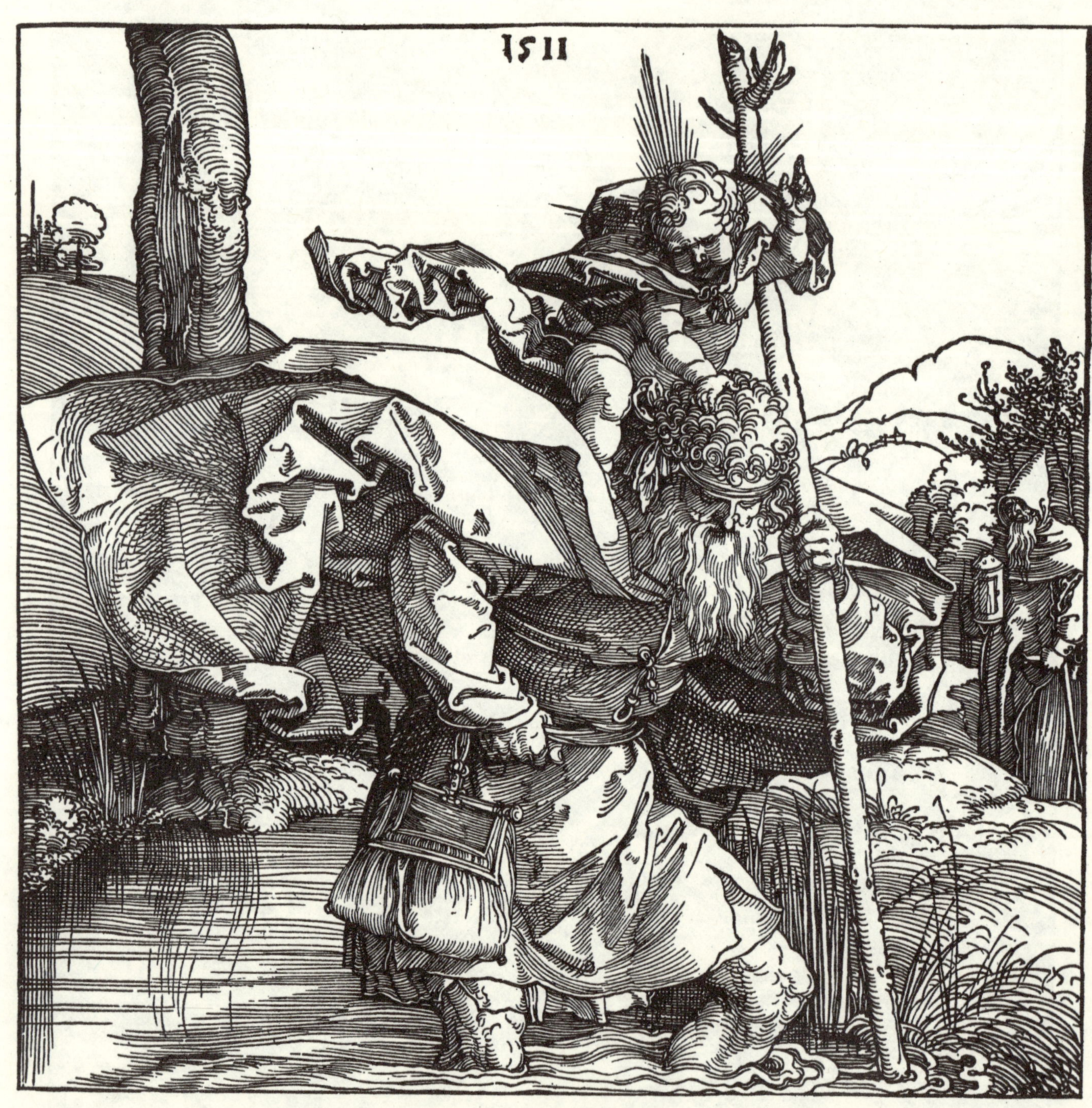

56. Saint Christopher

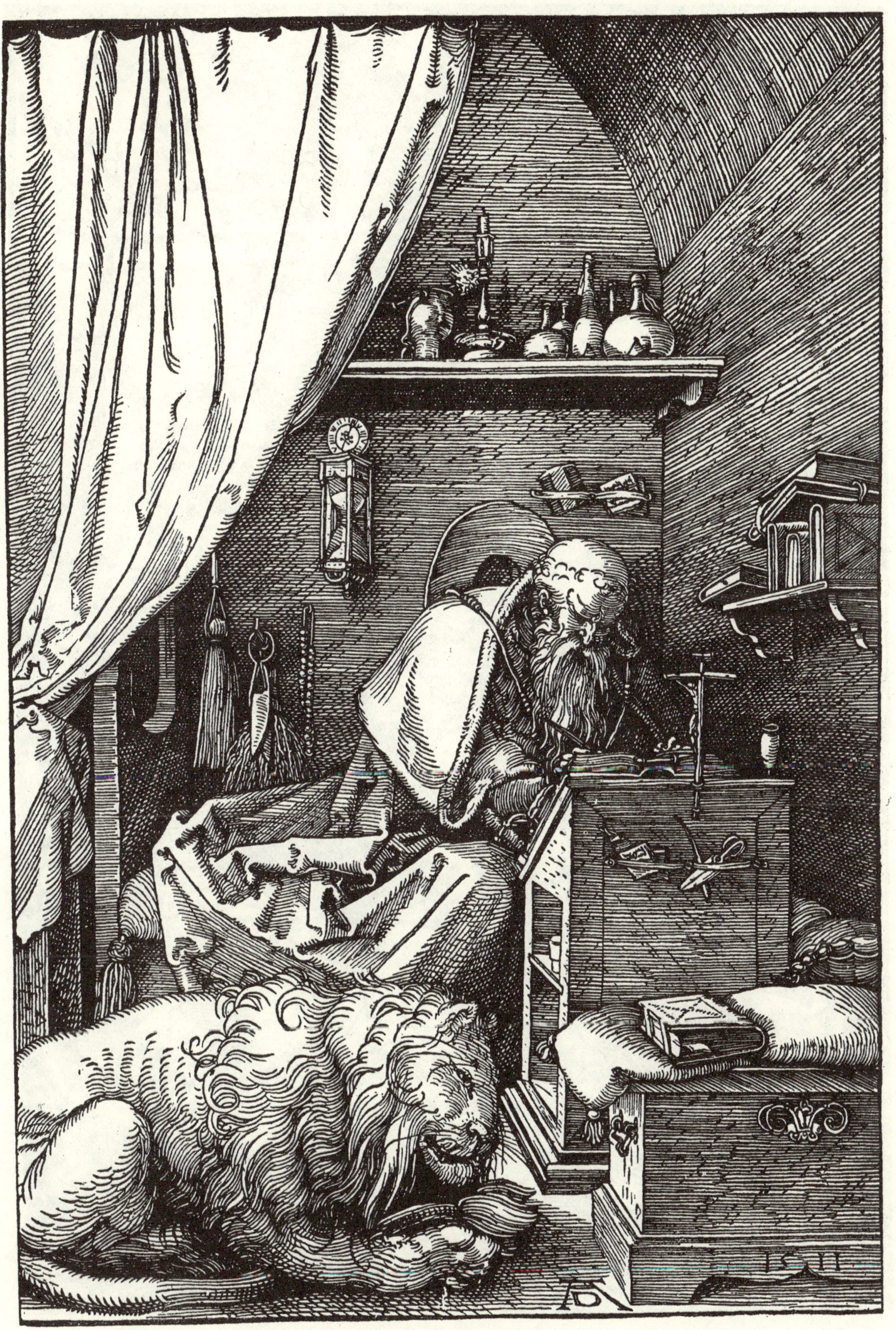

57. St. Jerome in His Cell

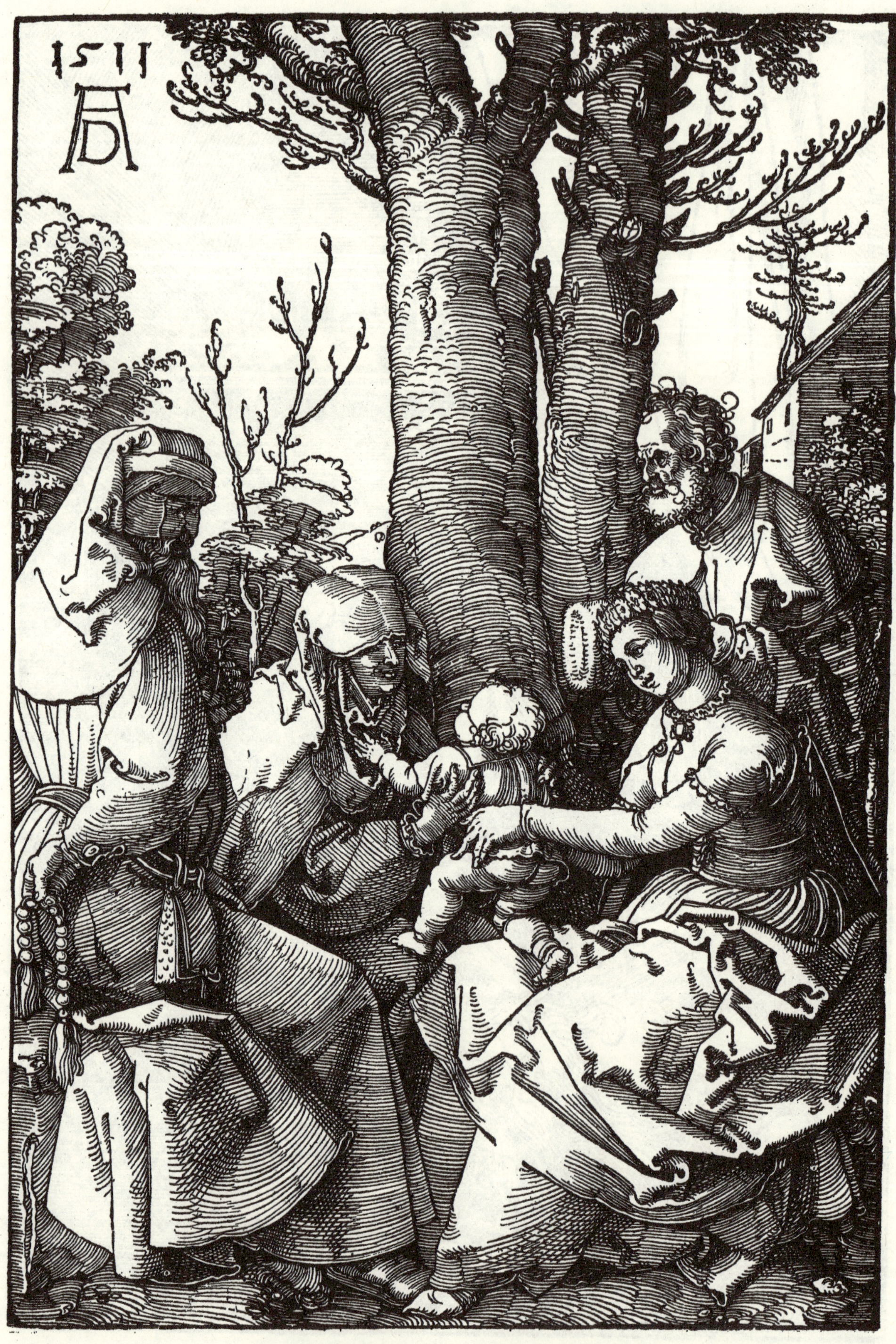

58. The Holy Family with Joachim and Anna

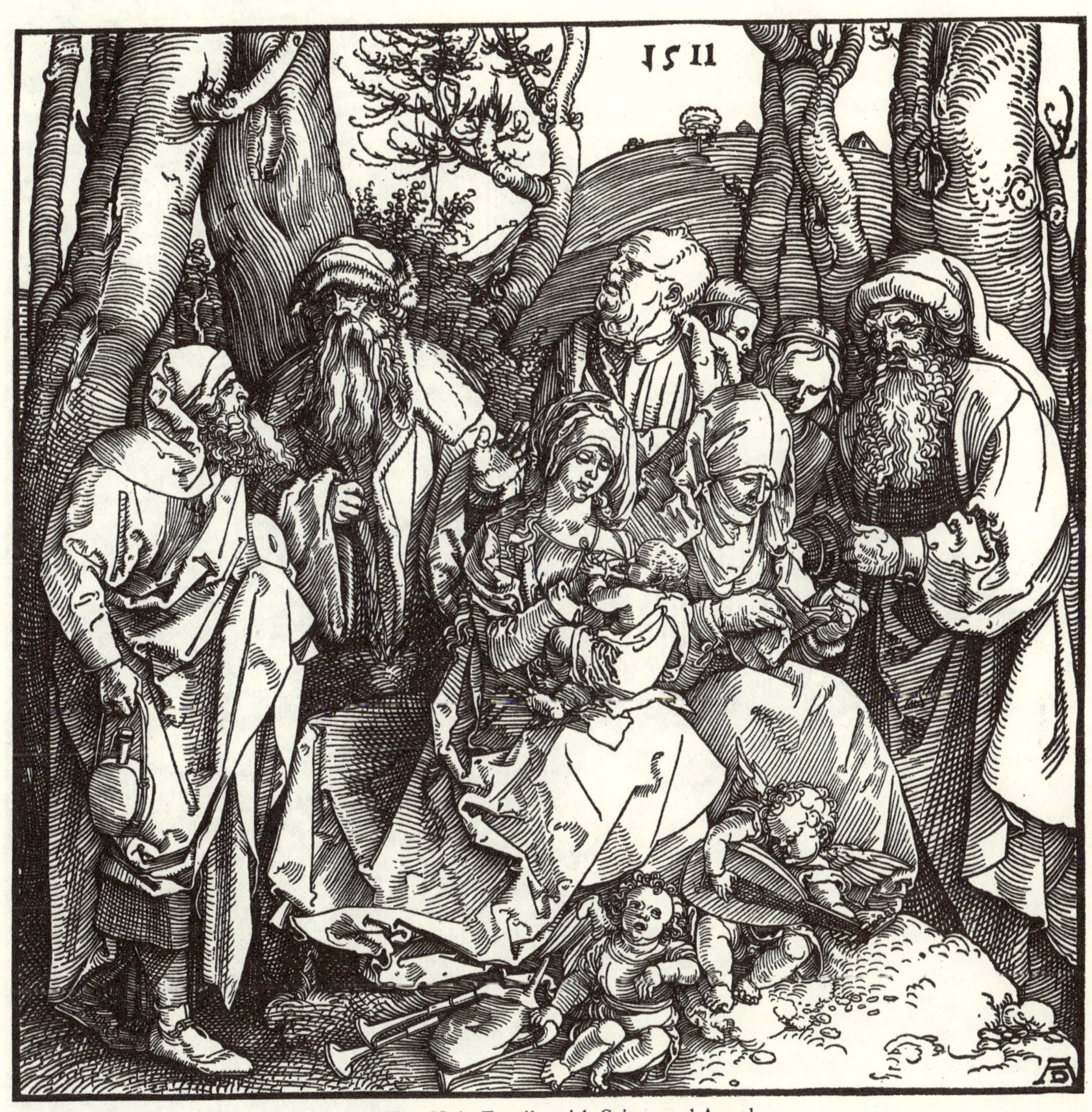

59. The Holy Family with Saints and Angels

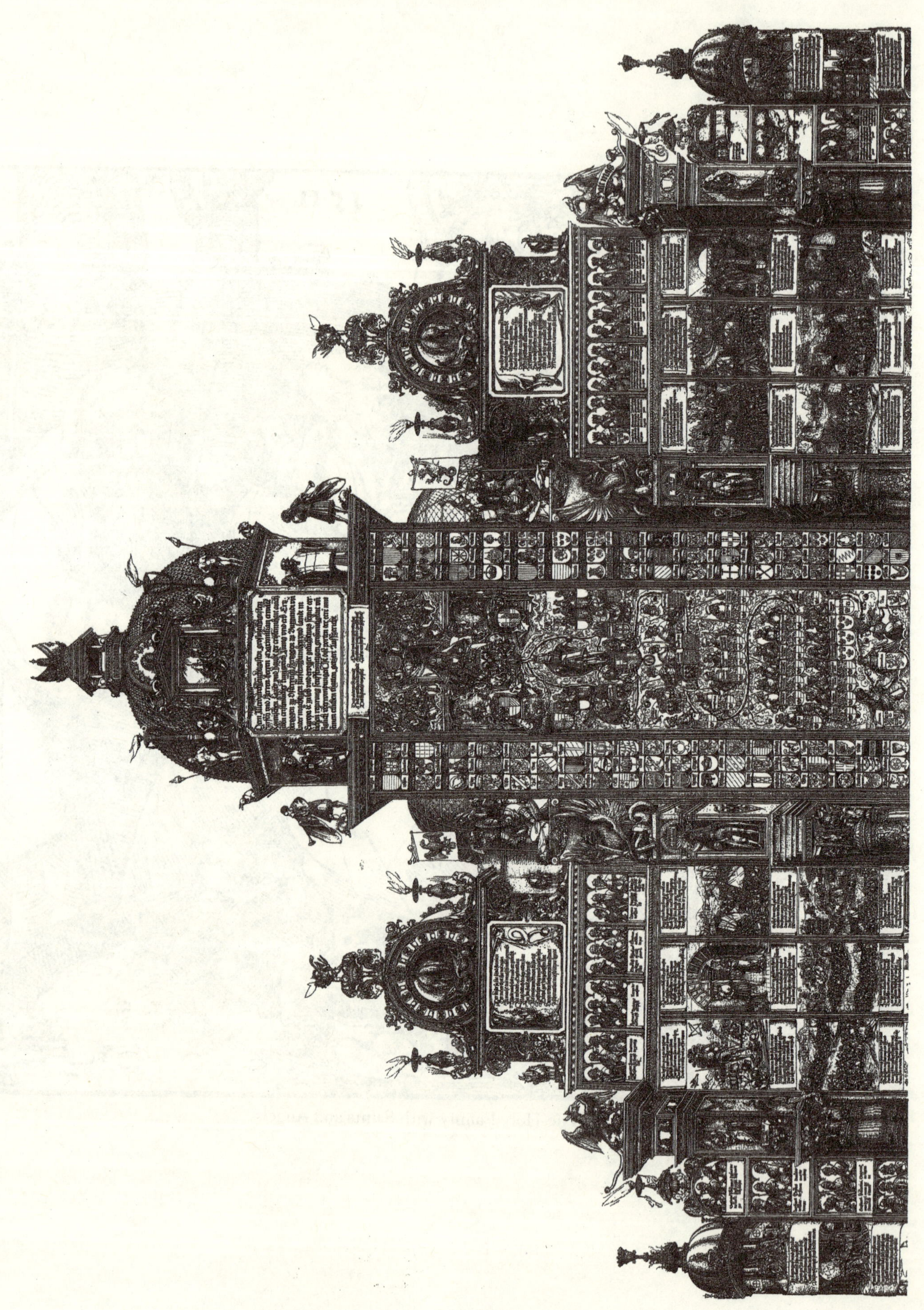

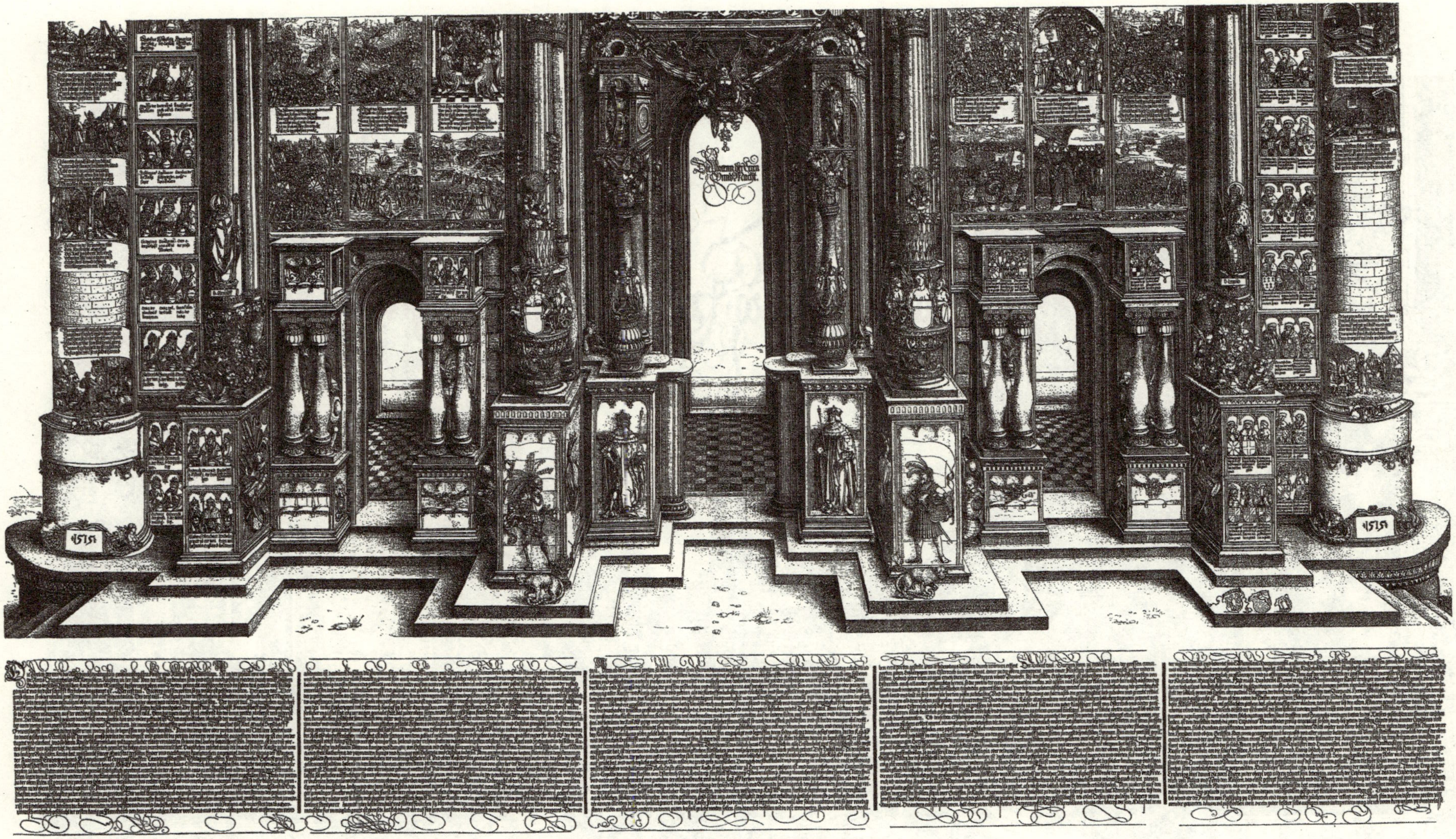

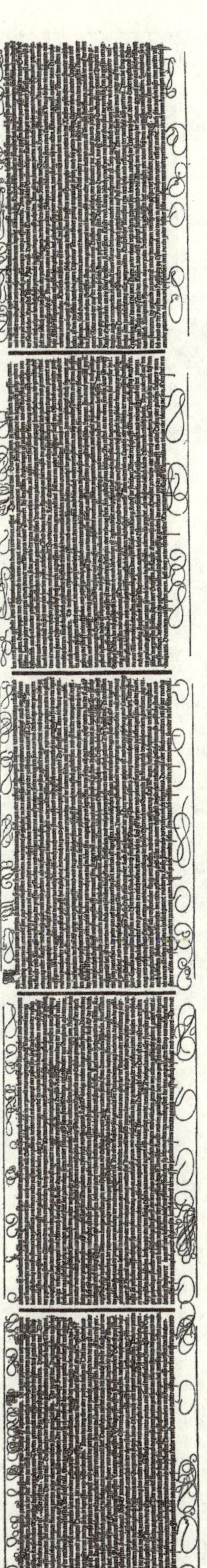

60. View of the Entire Triumphal Arch

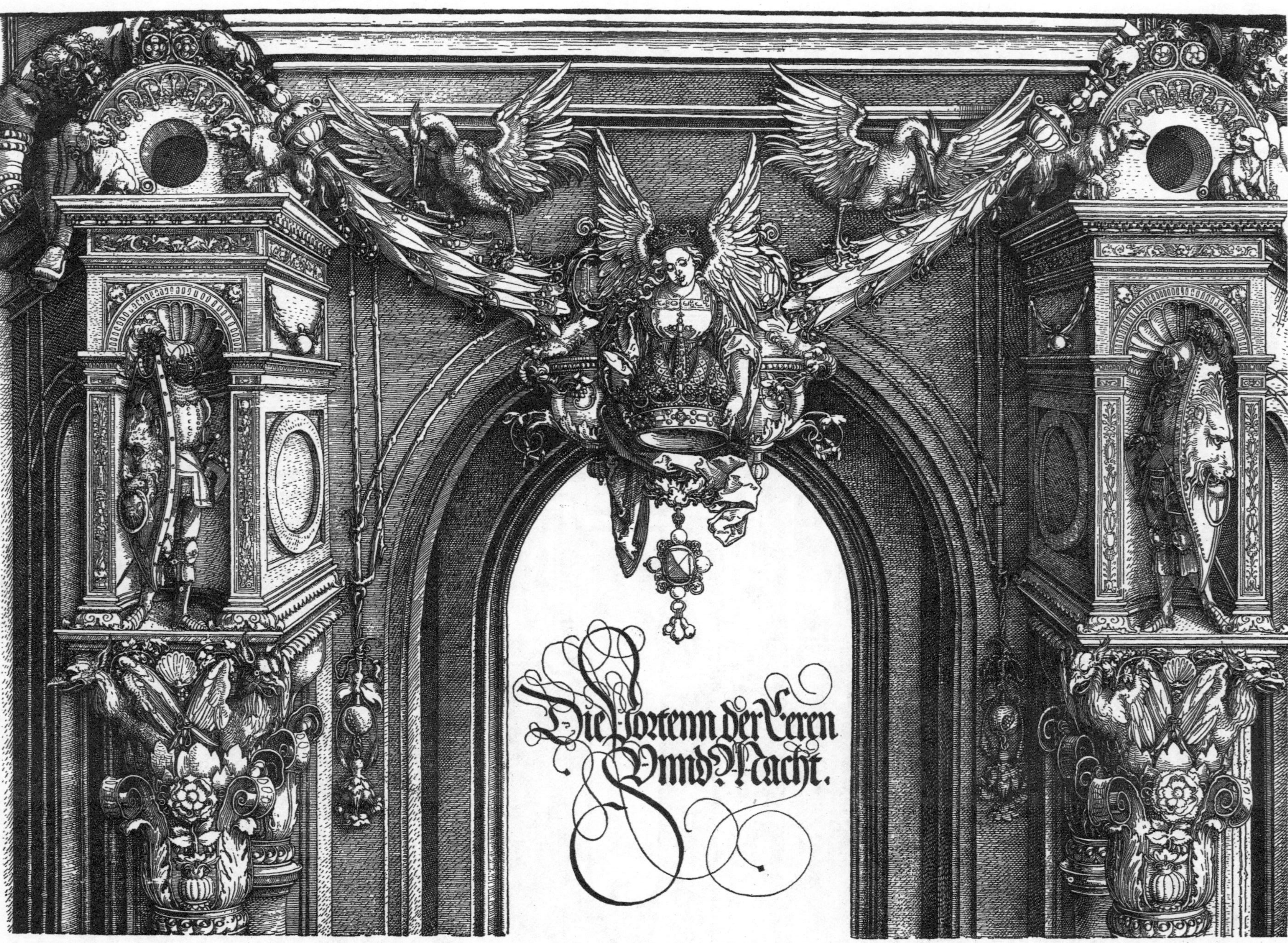

61. Upper part of the middle gateway: the gateway of Honour and Might

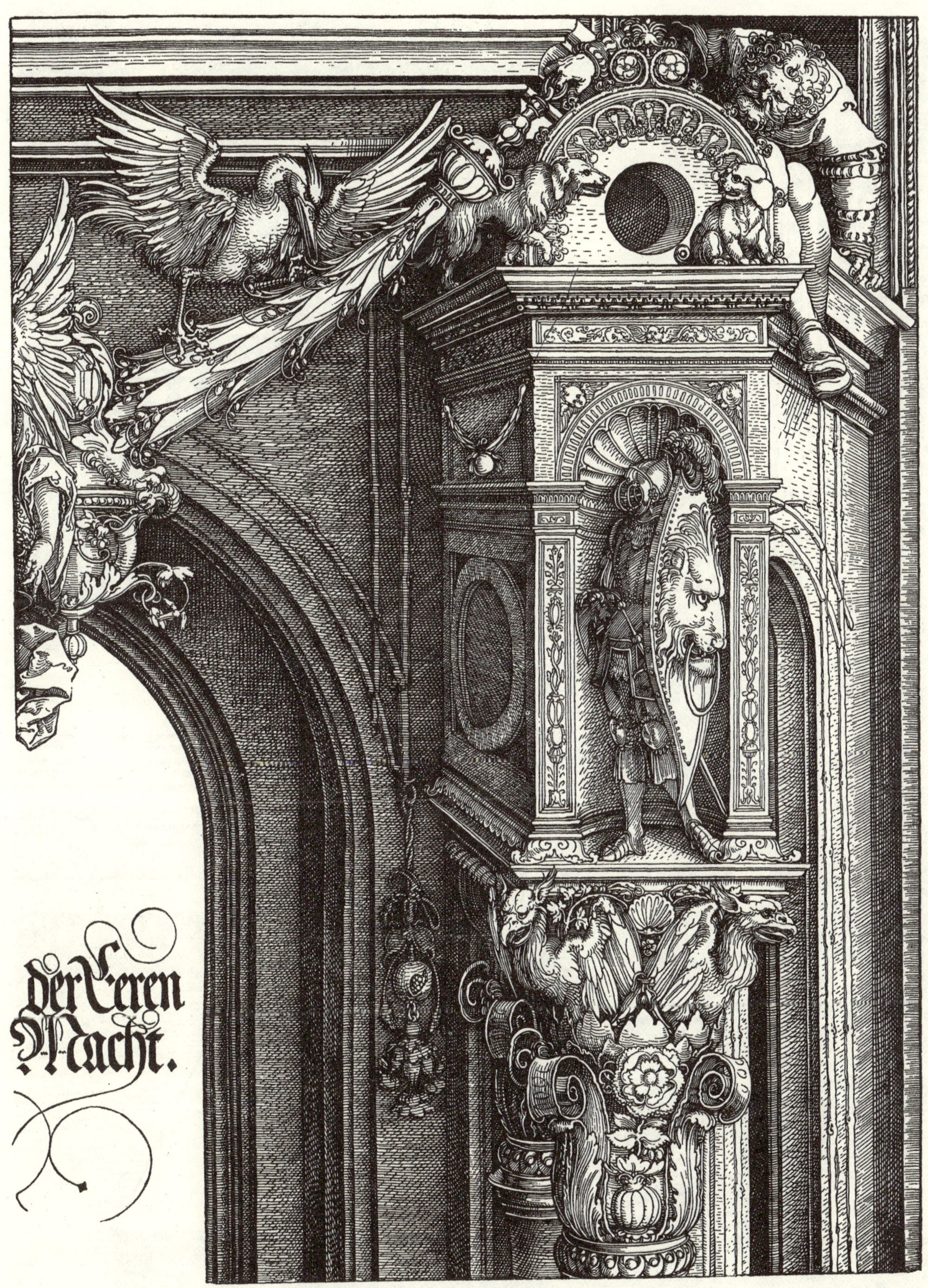

62. Part of the centre gateway in its original size

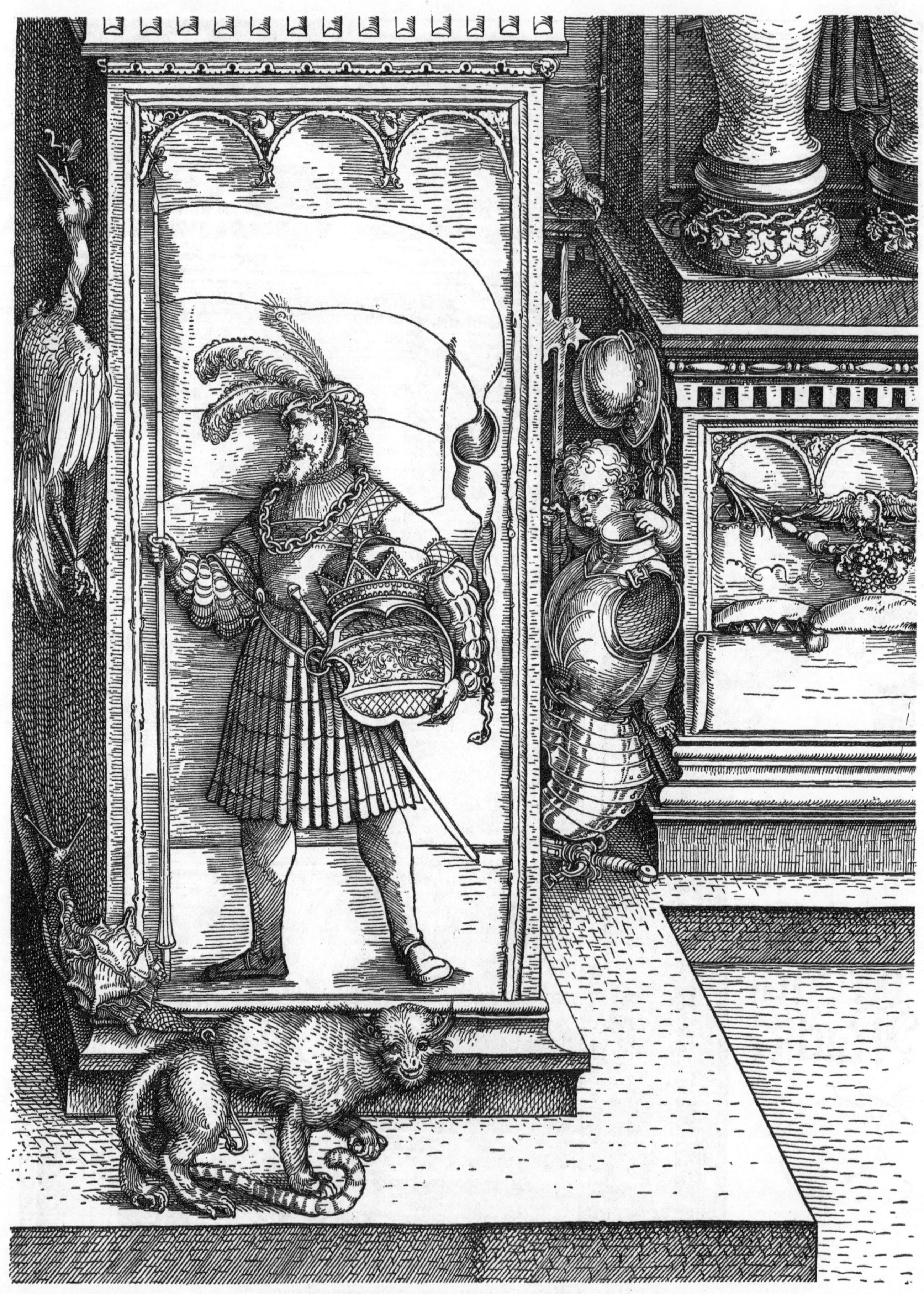

63. Pedestal of the right hand middle column

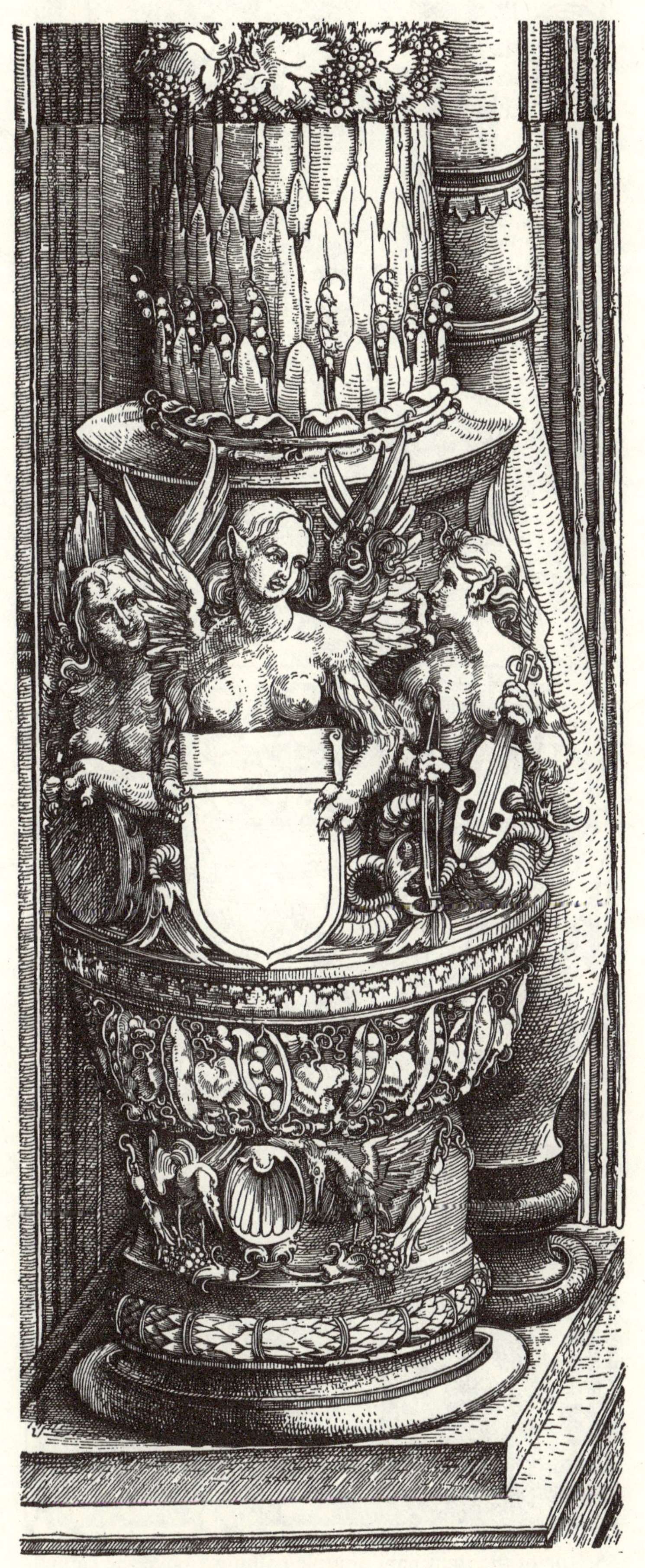

64. Base of the right hand middle column

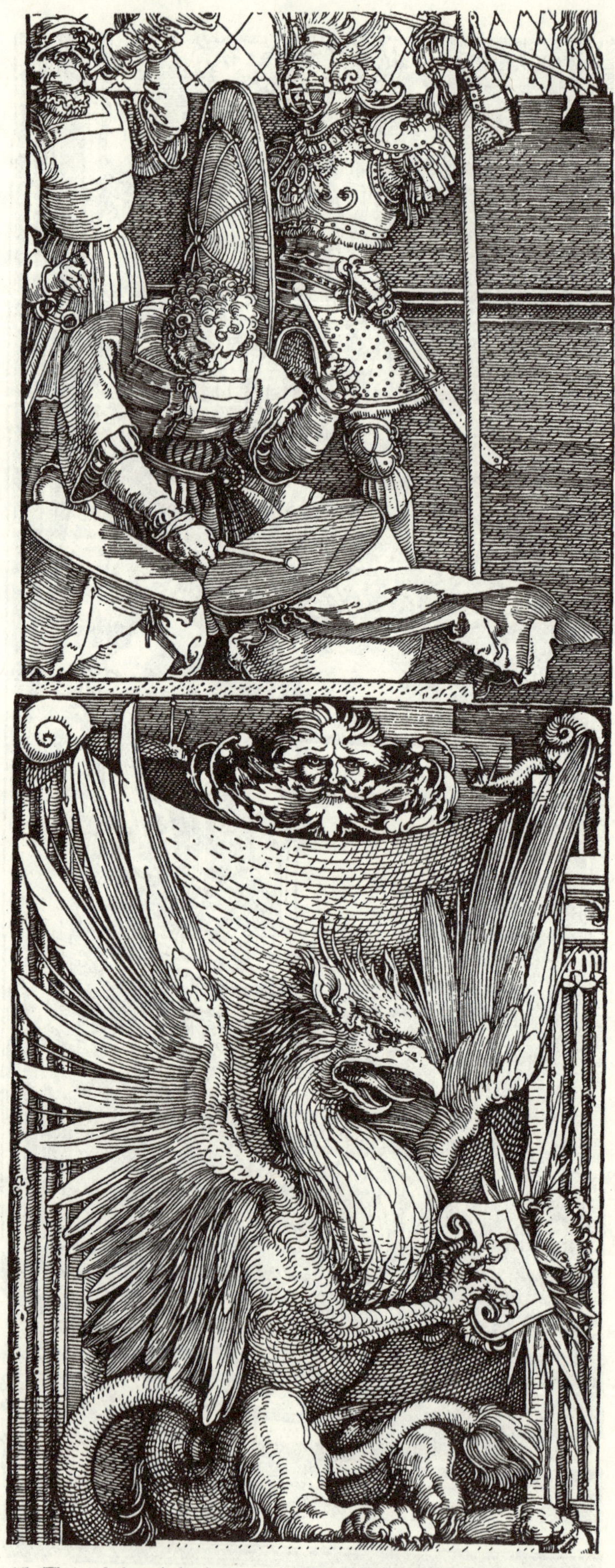

65. Top of the right hand middle column, above the capital and the ornamentation of the niche

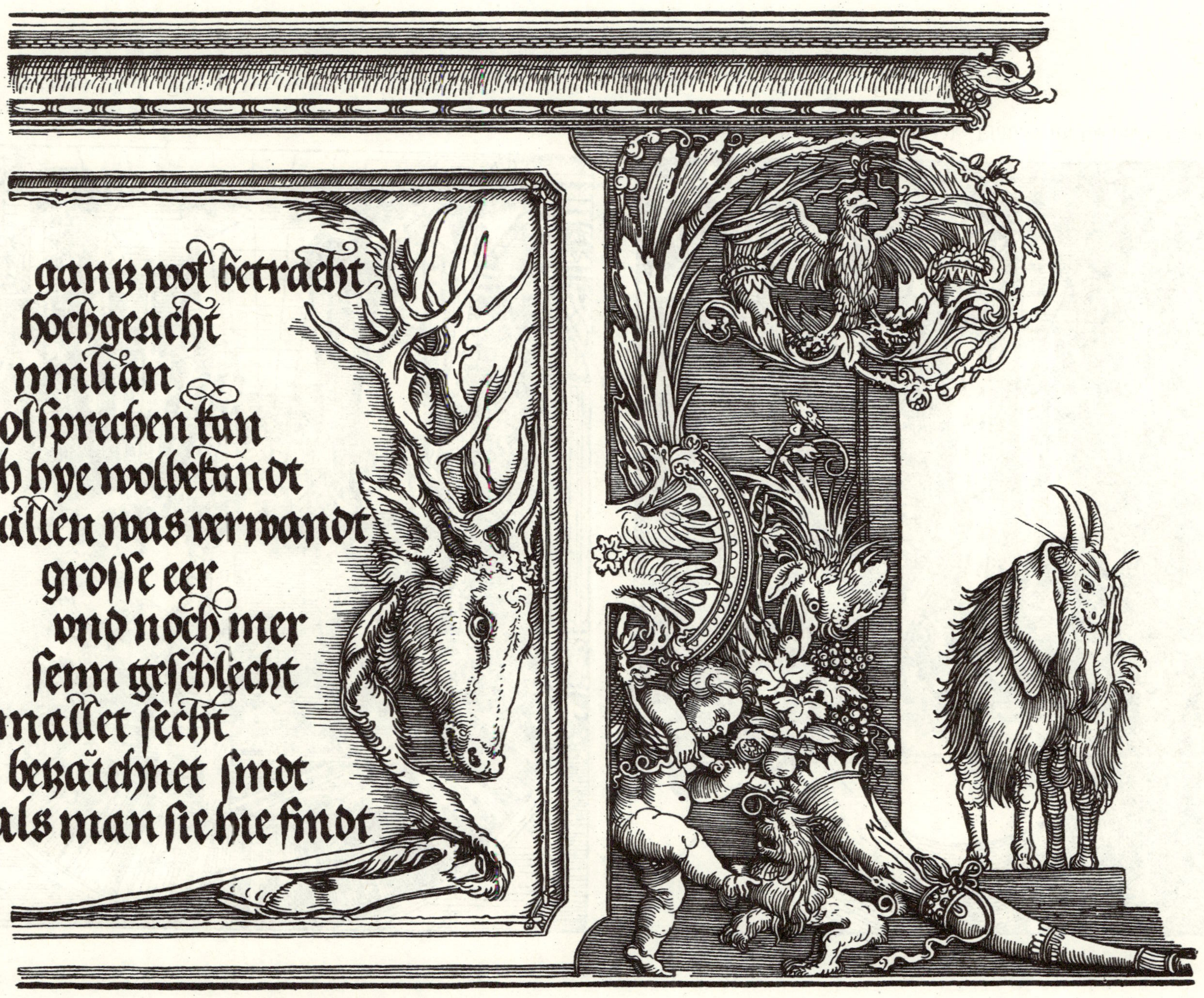

66. Inscription tablet with the stag's skin, from the uppermost section of the right wing

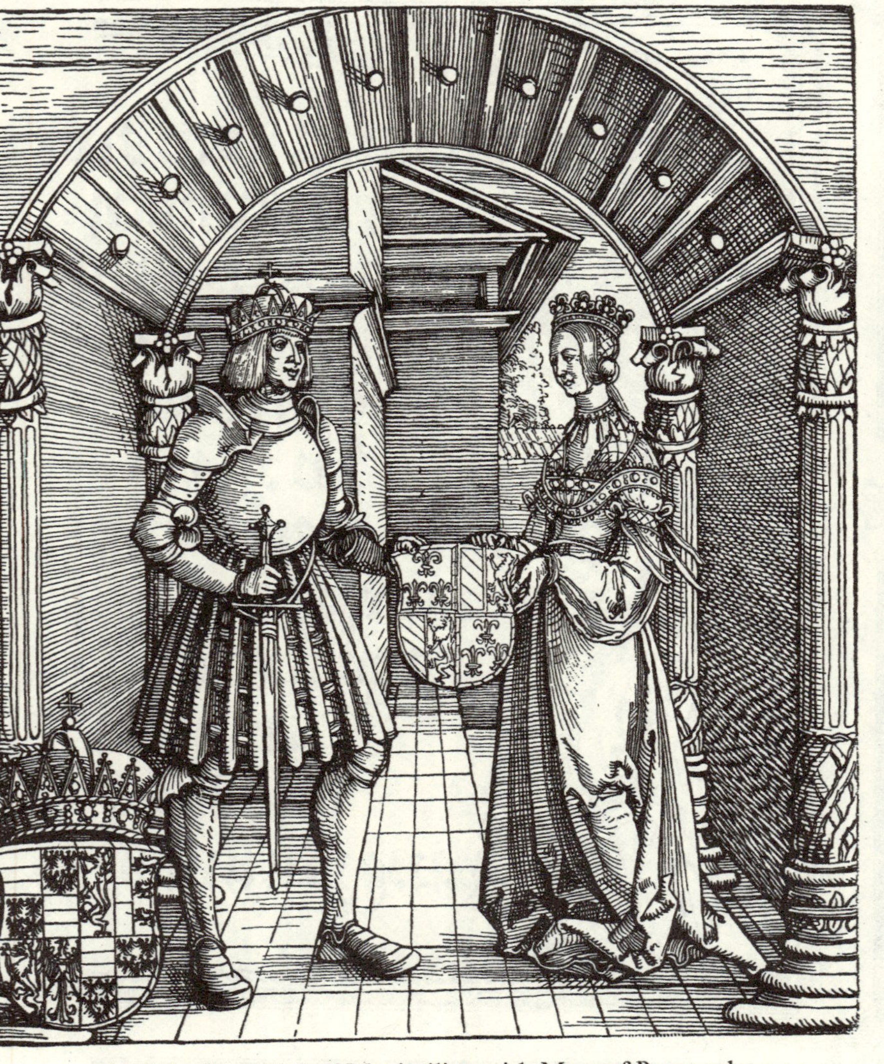

67. The Betrothal of Maximilian with Mary of Burgundy

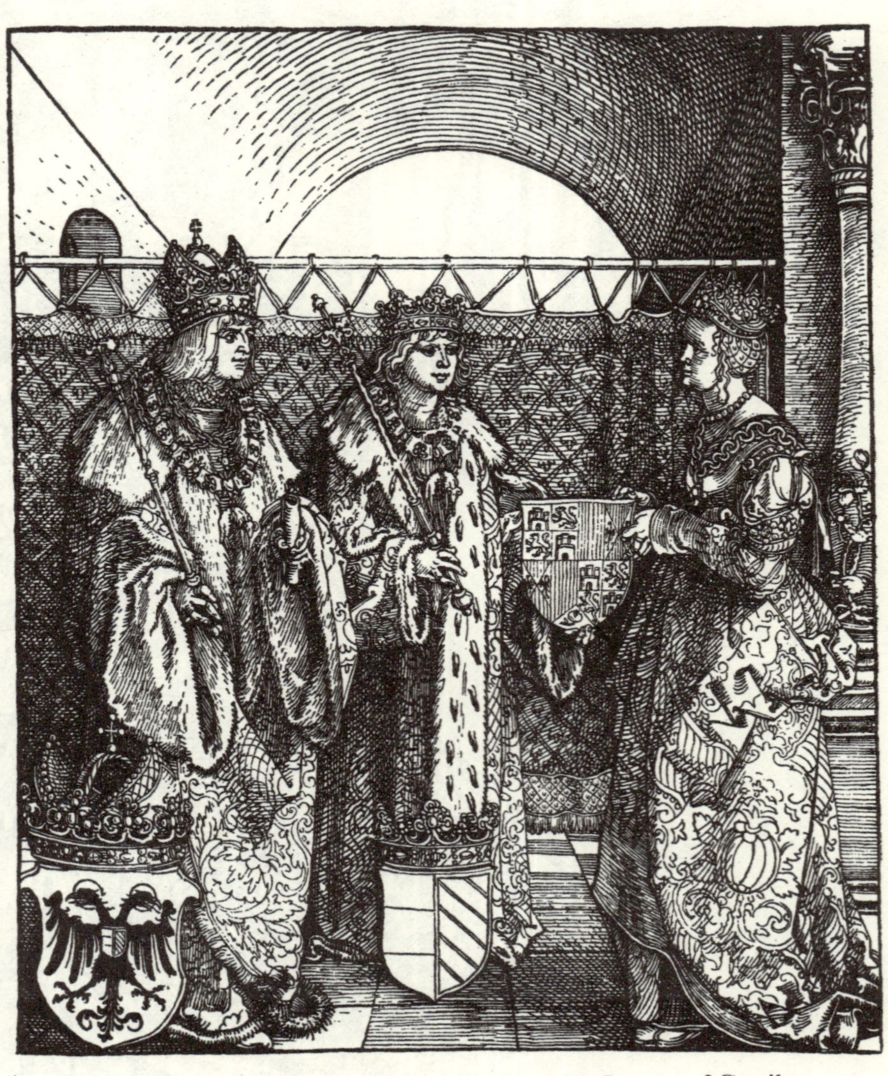

68. The Betrothal of Archduke Philip with Joanna of Castile

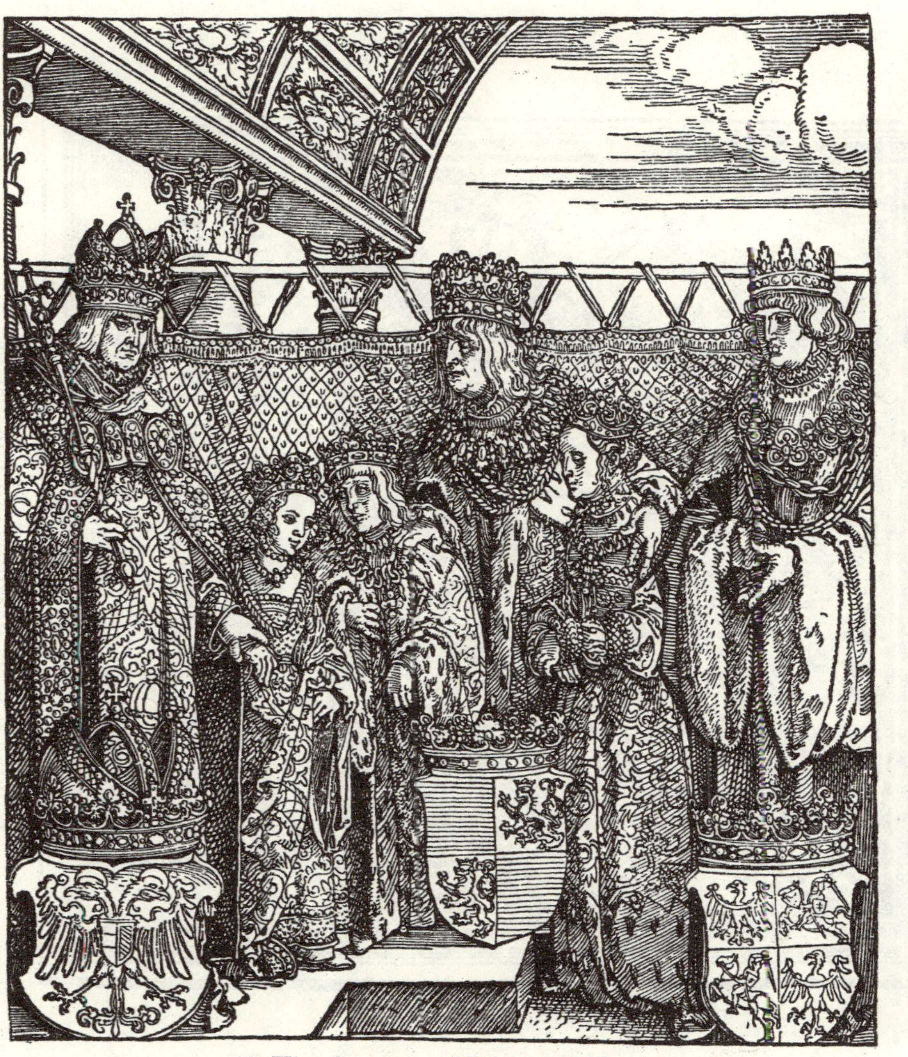

69. The Congress of Princes of Vienna

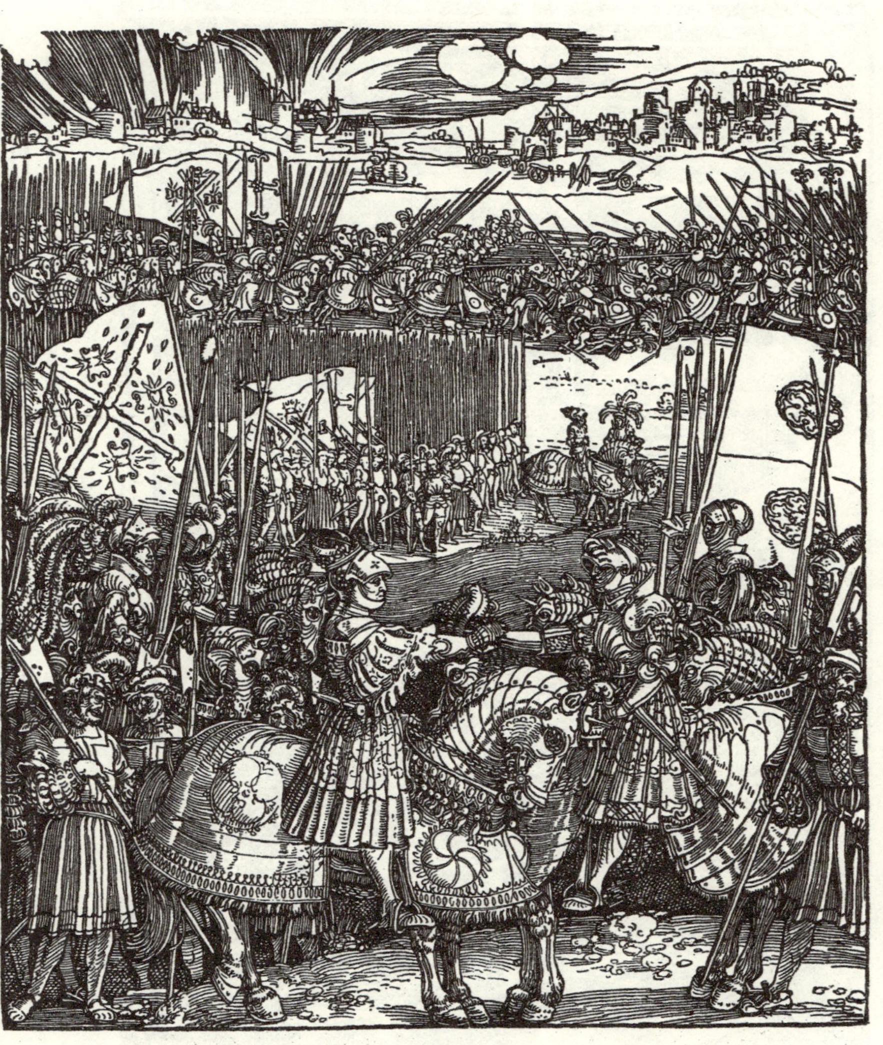

70. The Meeting after the Battle of the Spurs

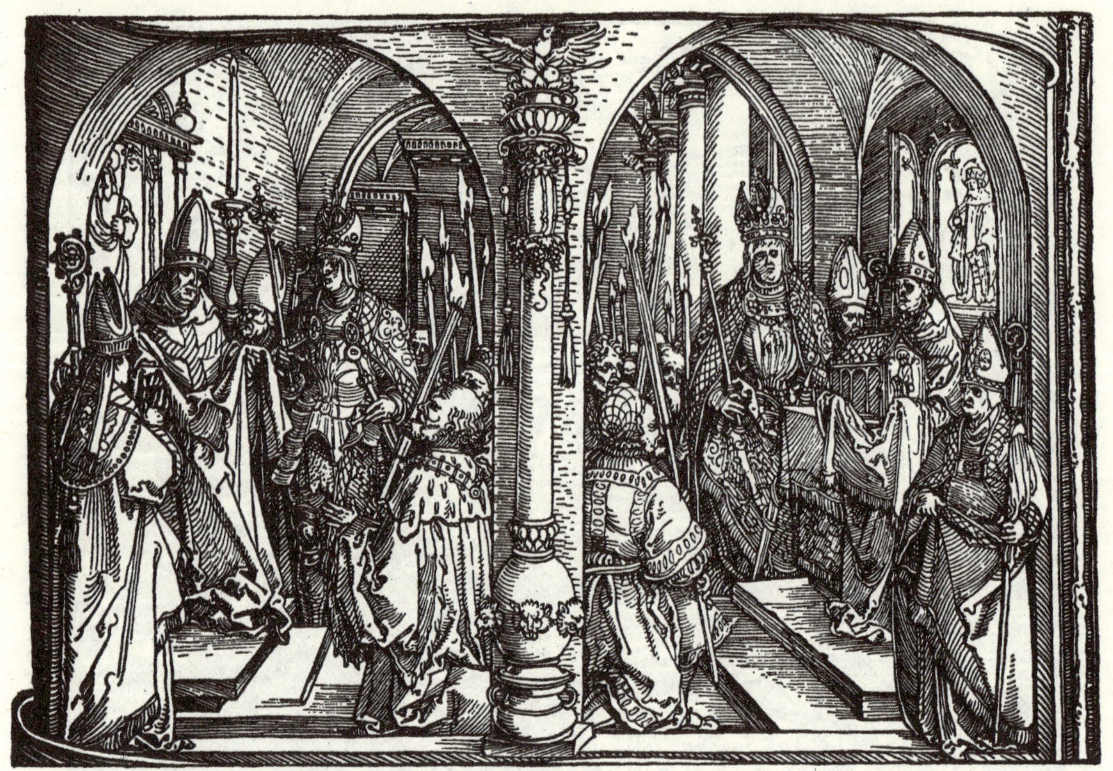

71. The Sacred Coat of Trier

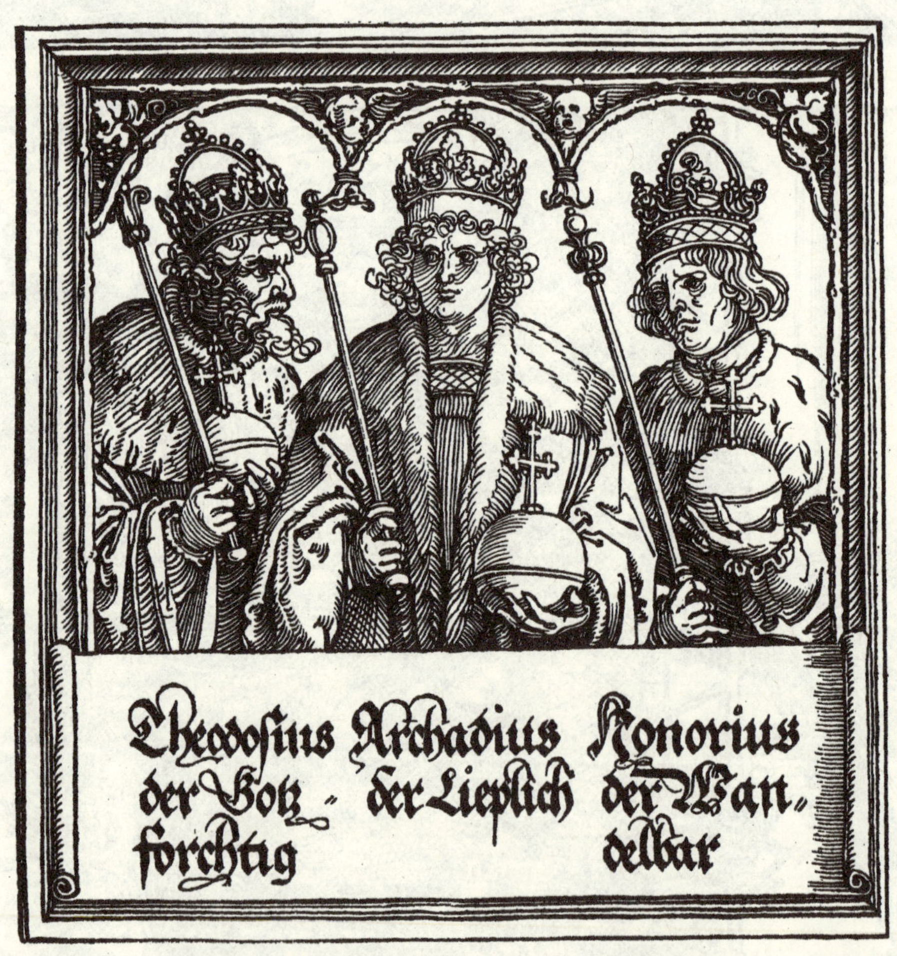

72. Fourth set of the Busts of Emperors, left side

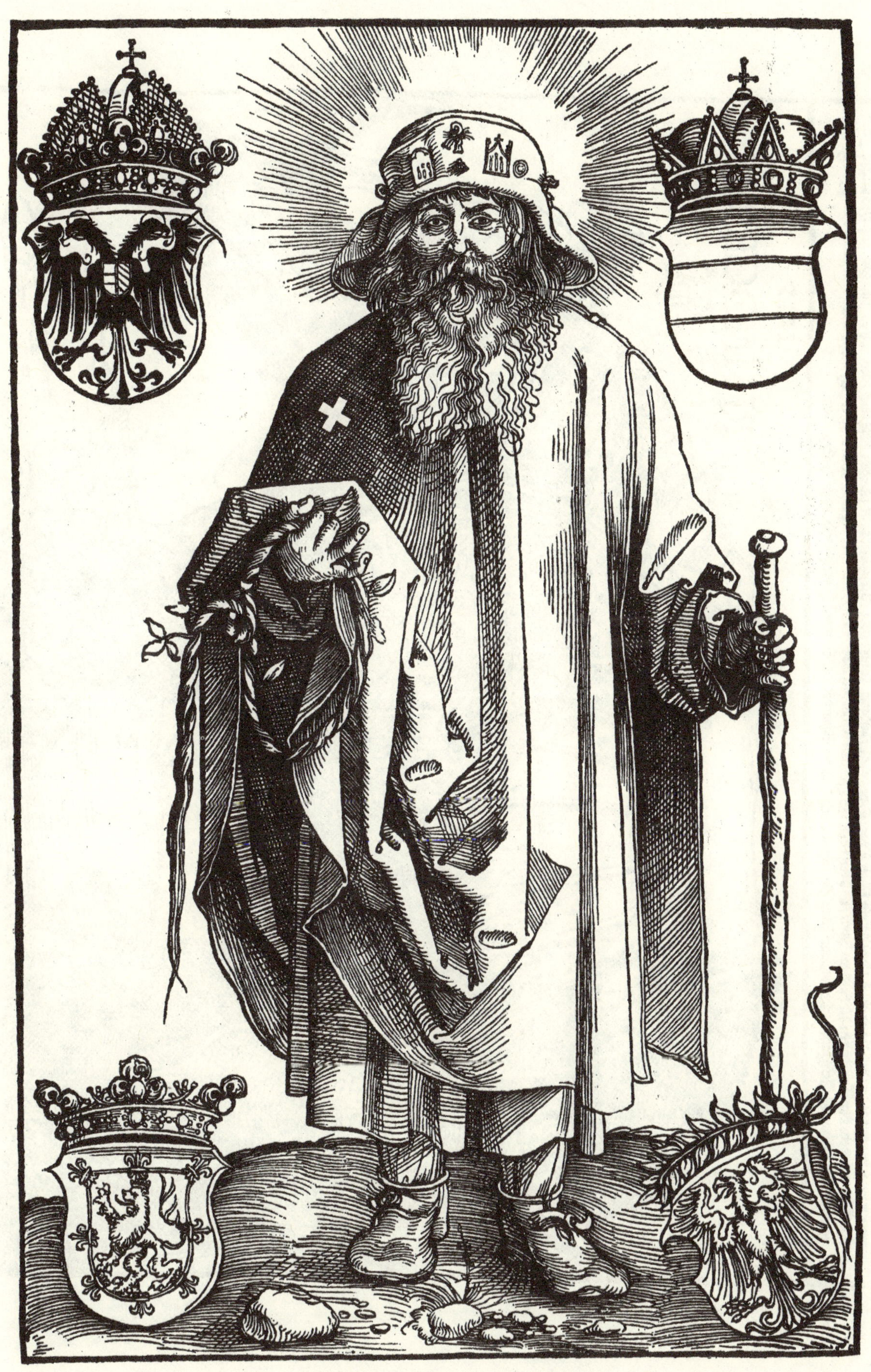

73. Saint Coloman as a Pilgrim

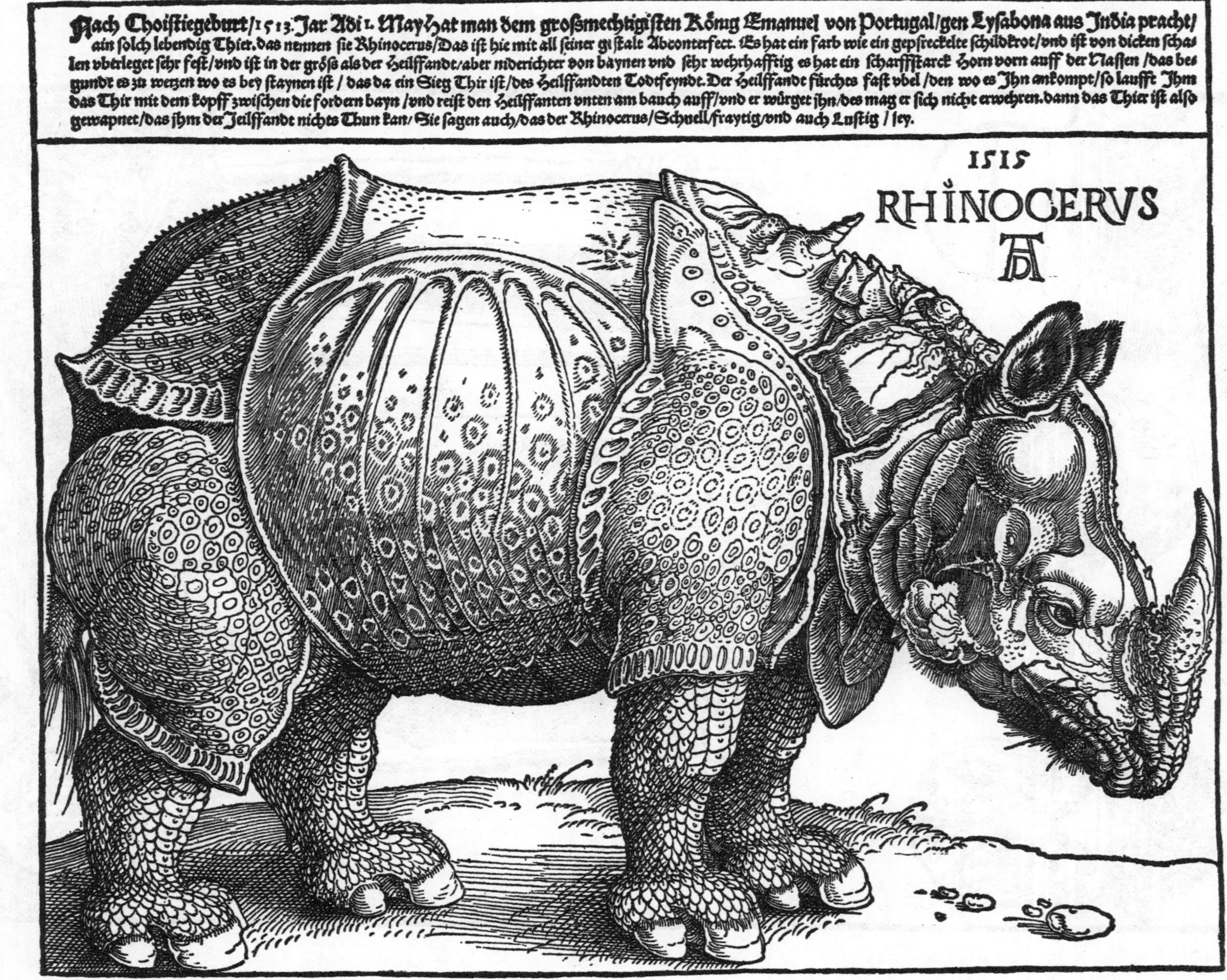

74. The Rhinoceros

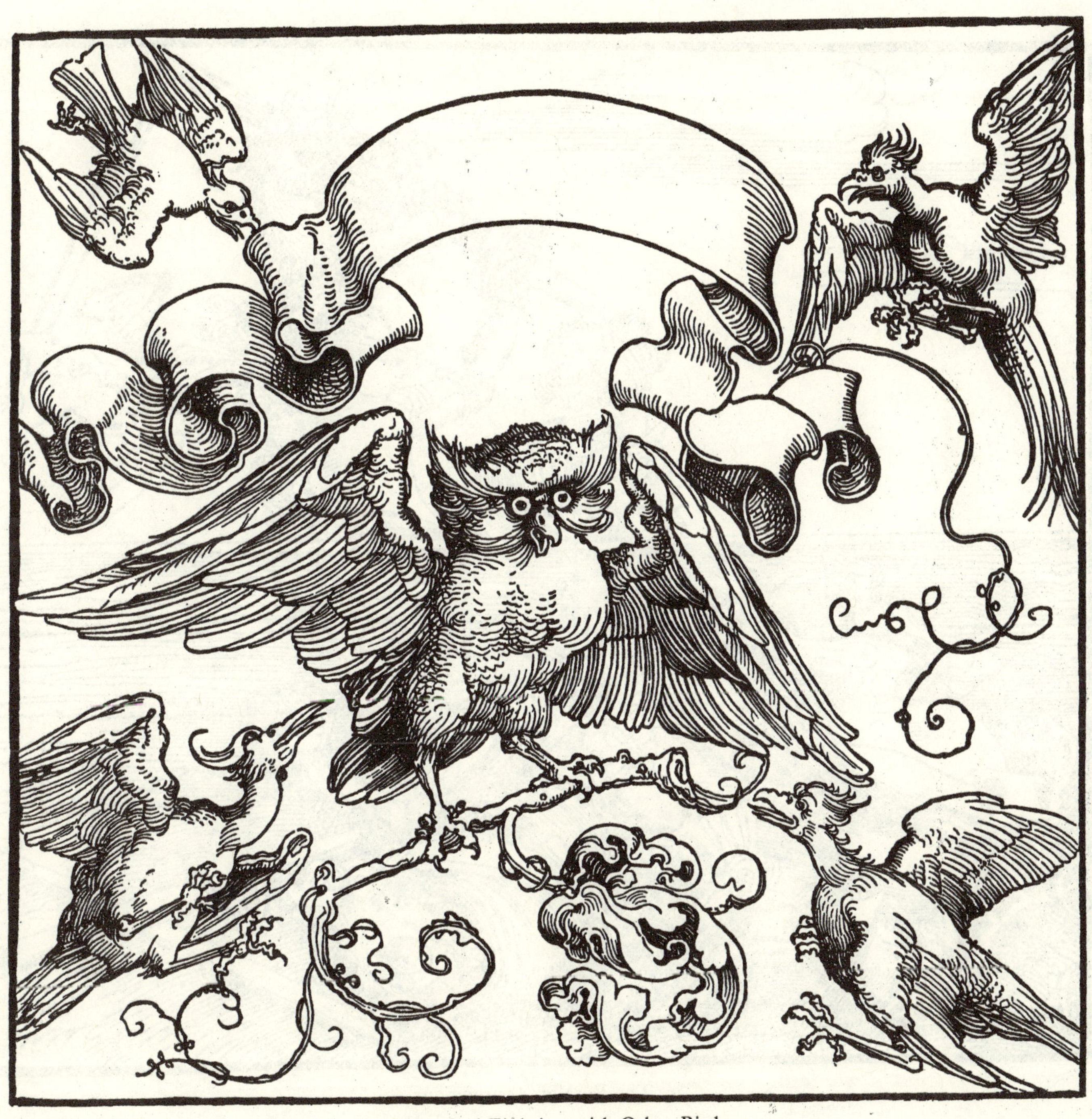

75. An Owl Fighting with Other Birds

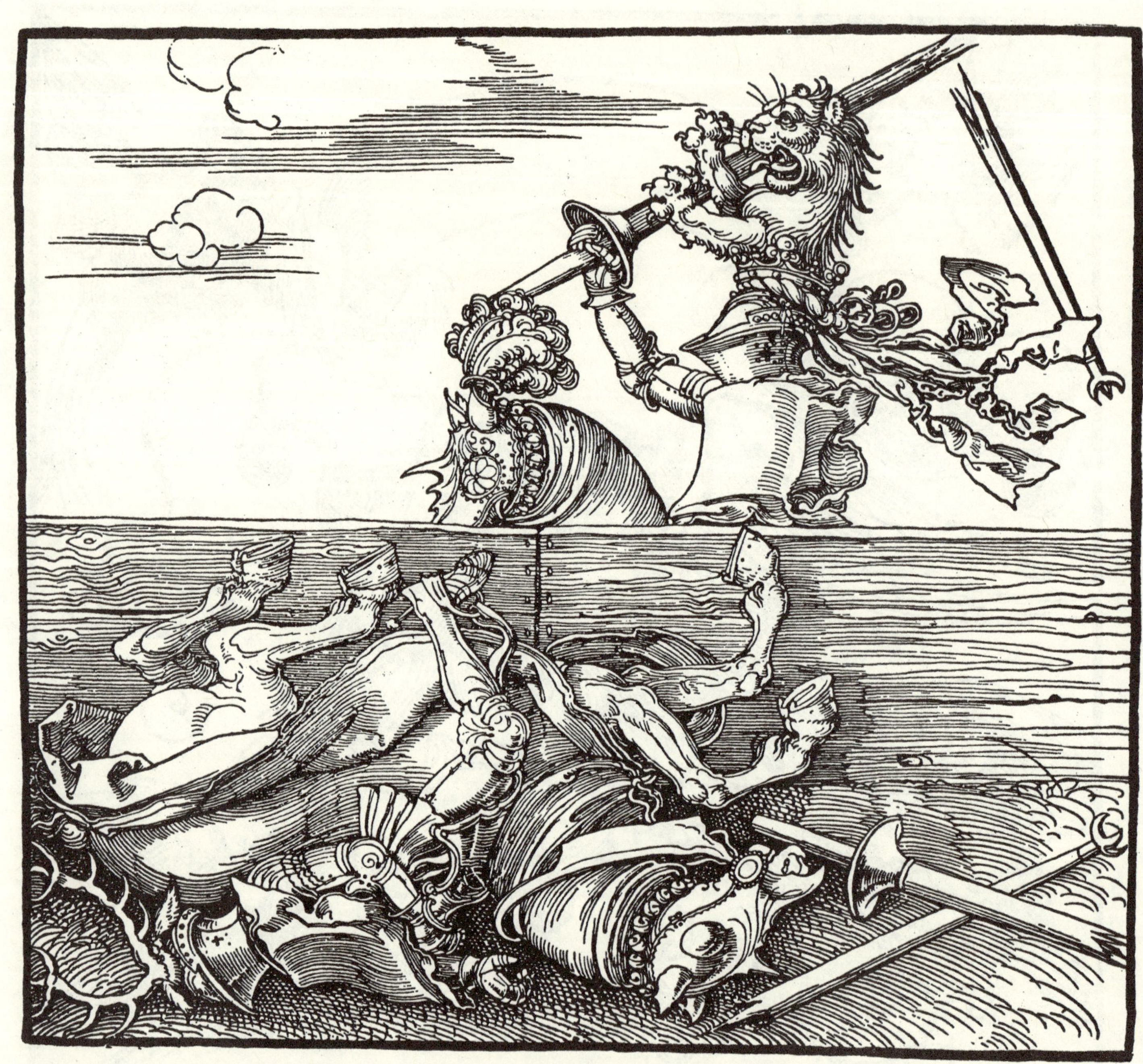

76. The Foreign Tournament

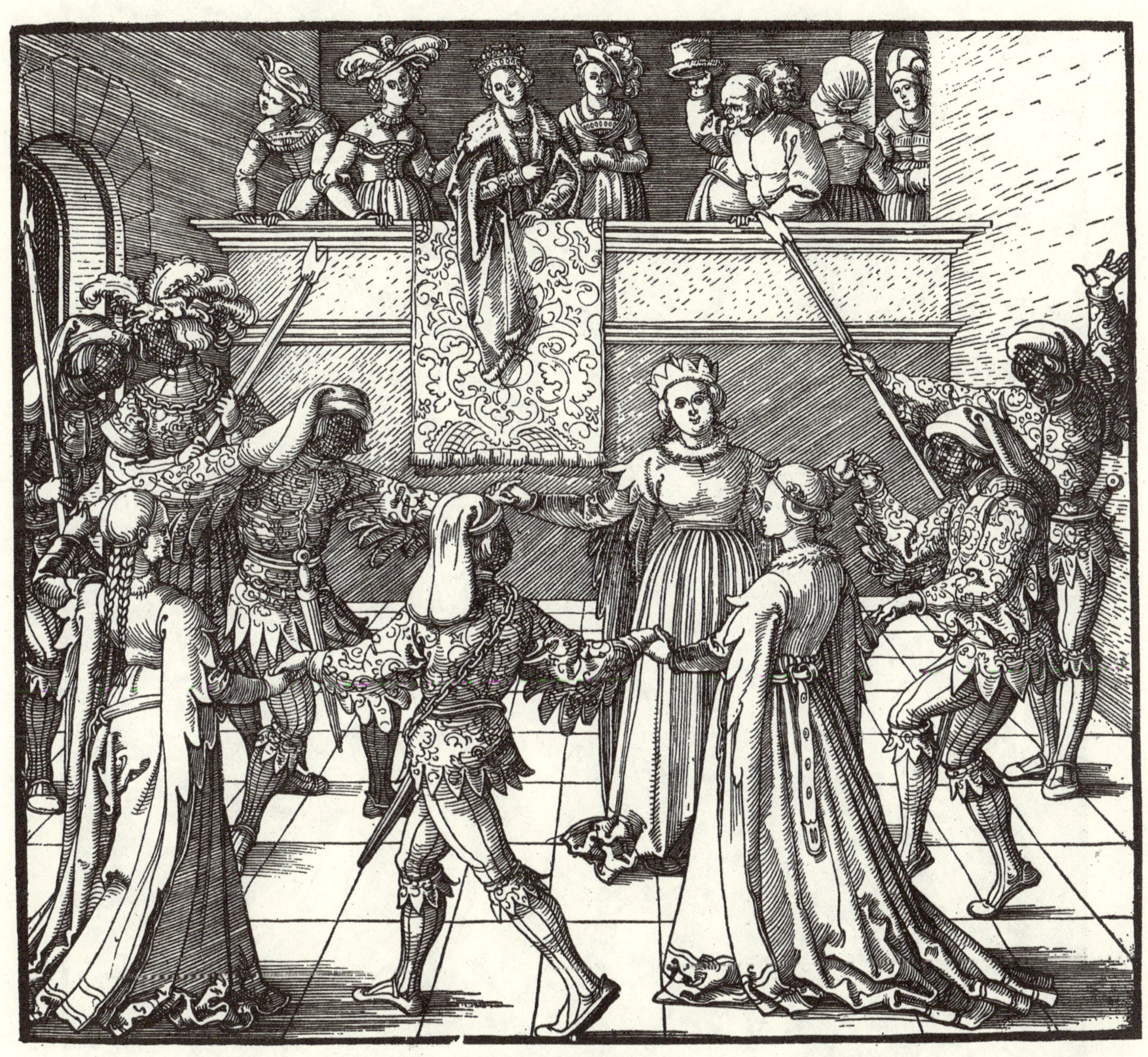

77. The Masquerade

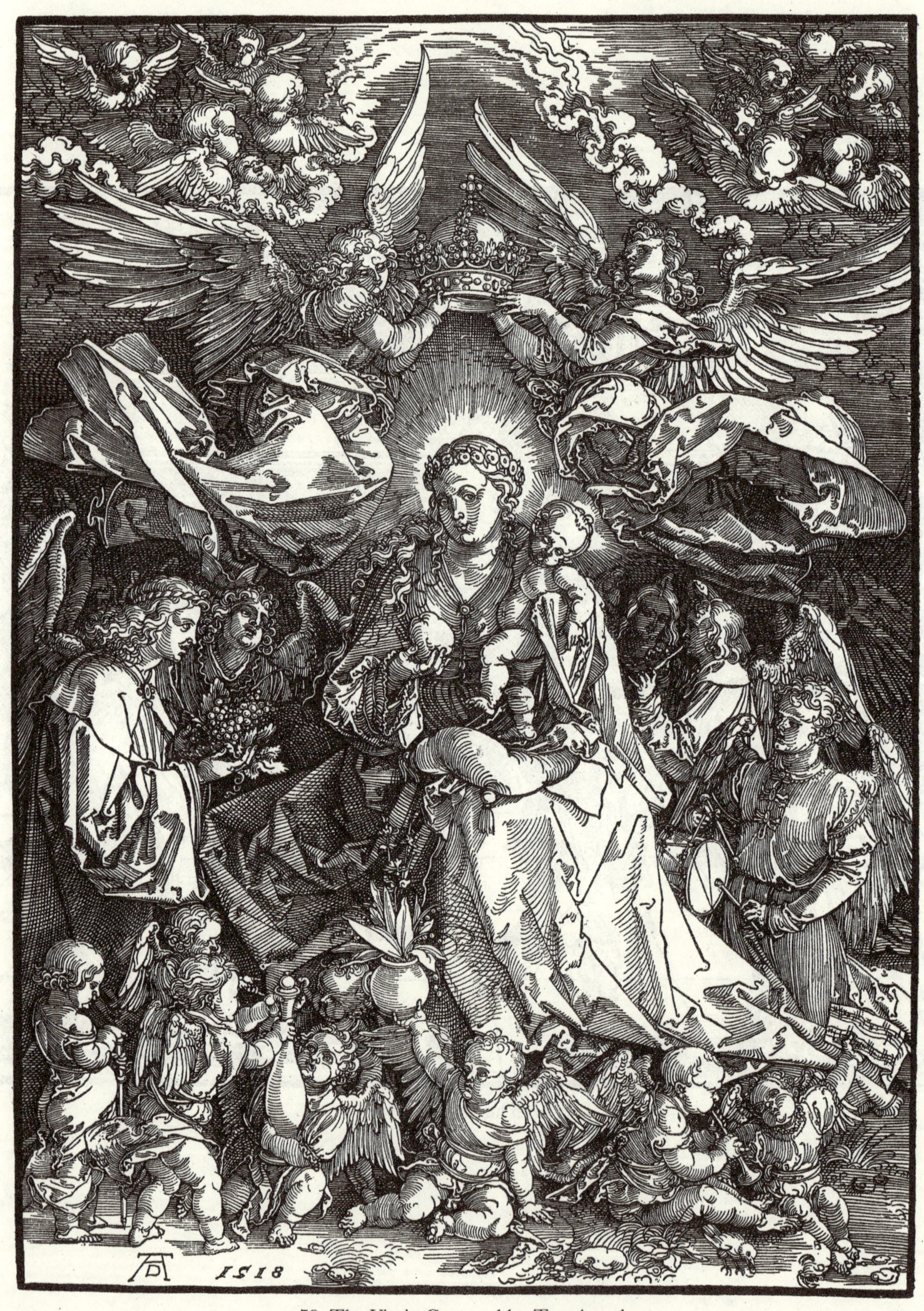

78. The Virgin Crowned by Two Angels

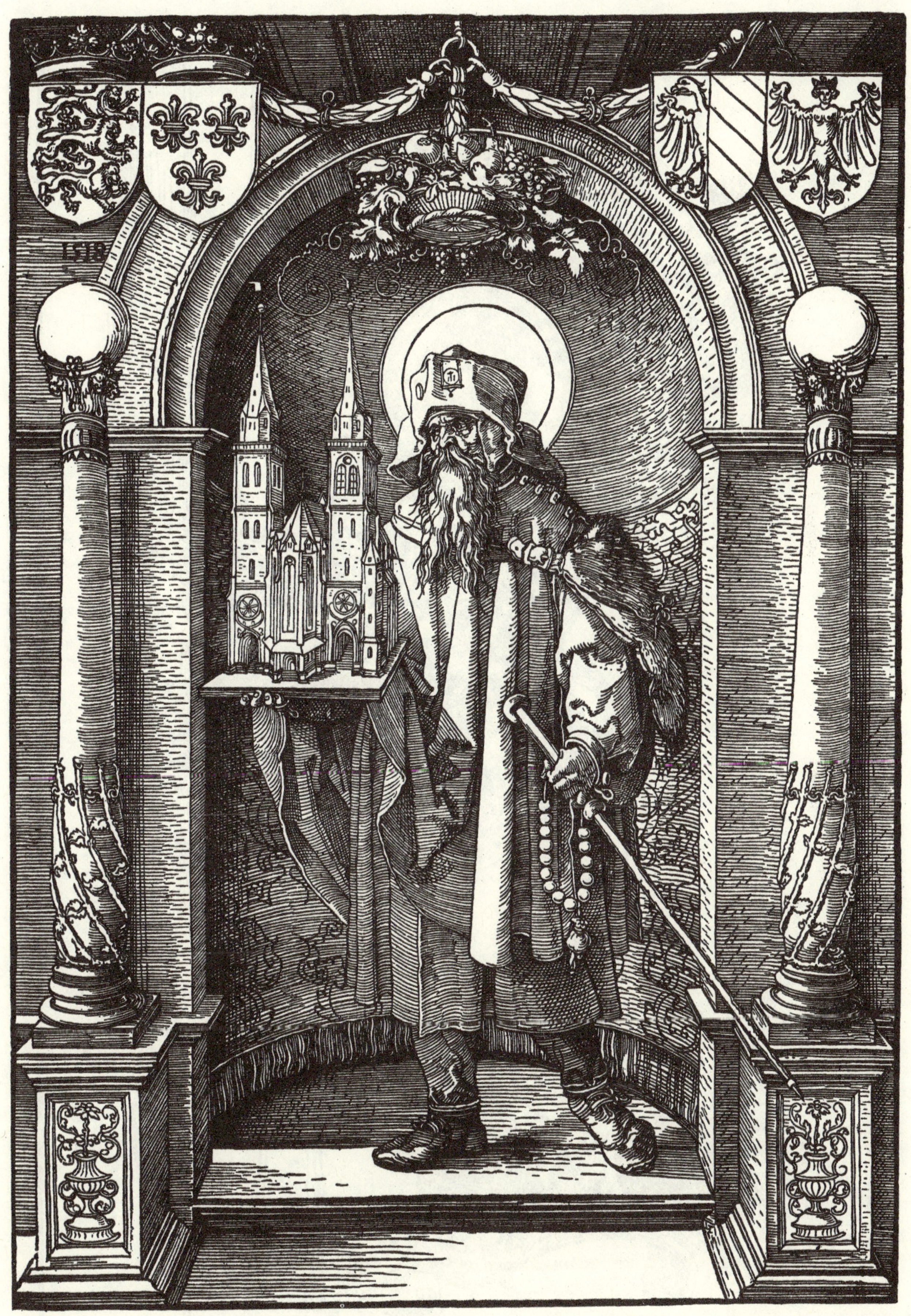

79. Saint Sebald in the Niche

80. Victory Guiding the Triumphal Car

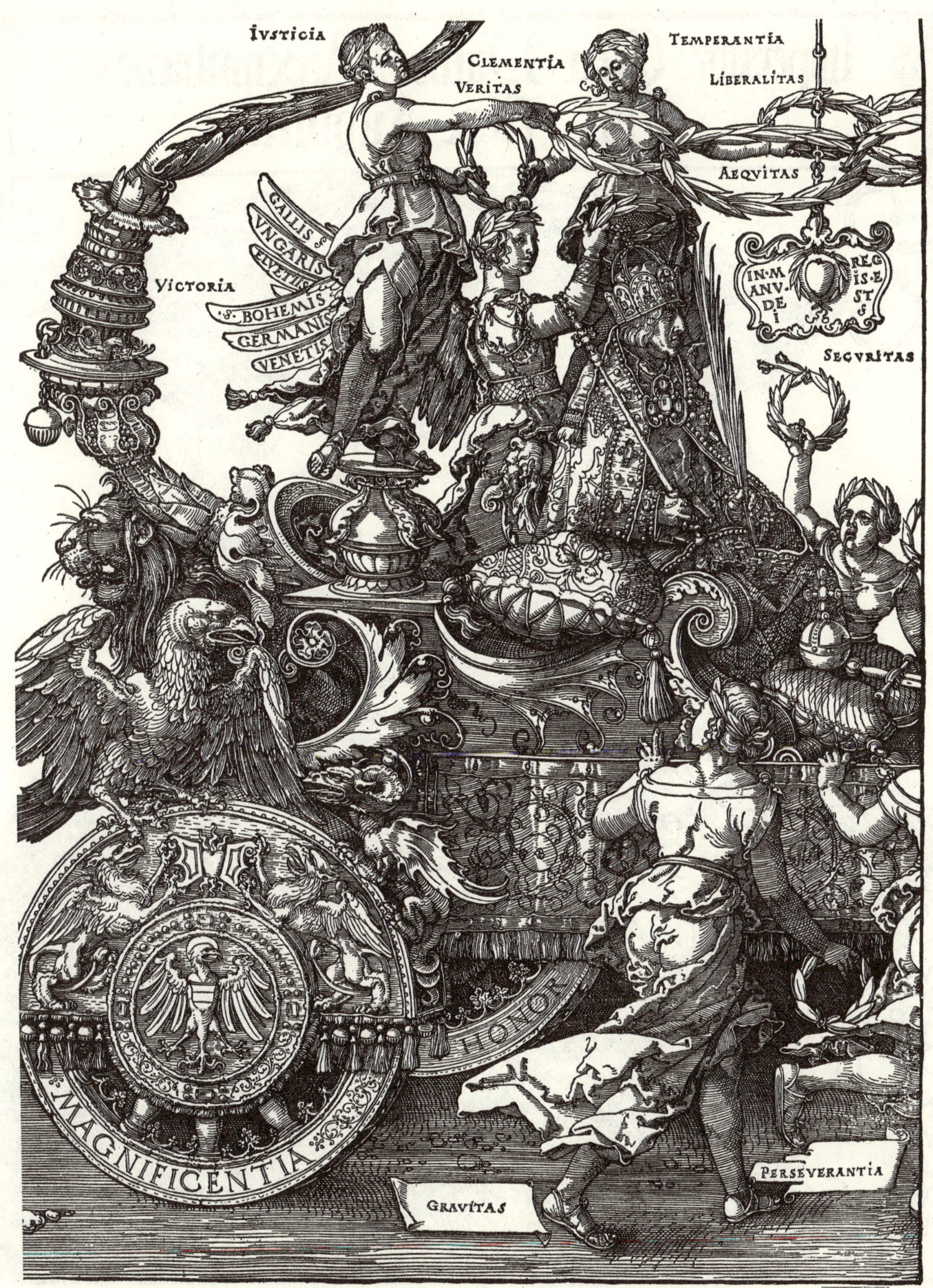

81. Back Part of the Imperial Car in Original Size

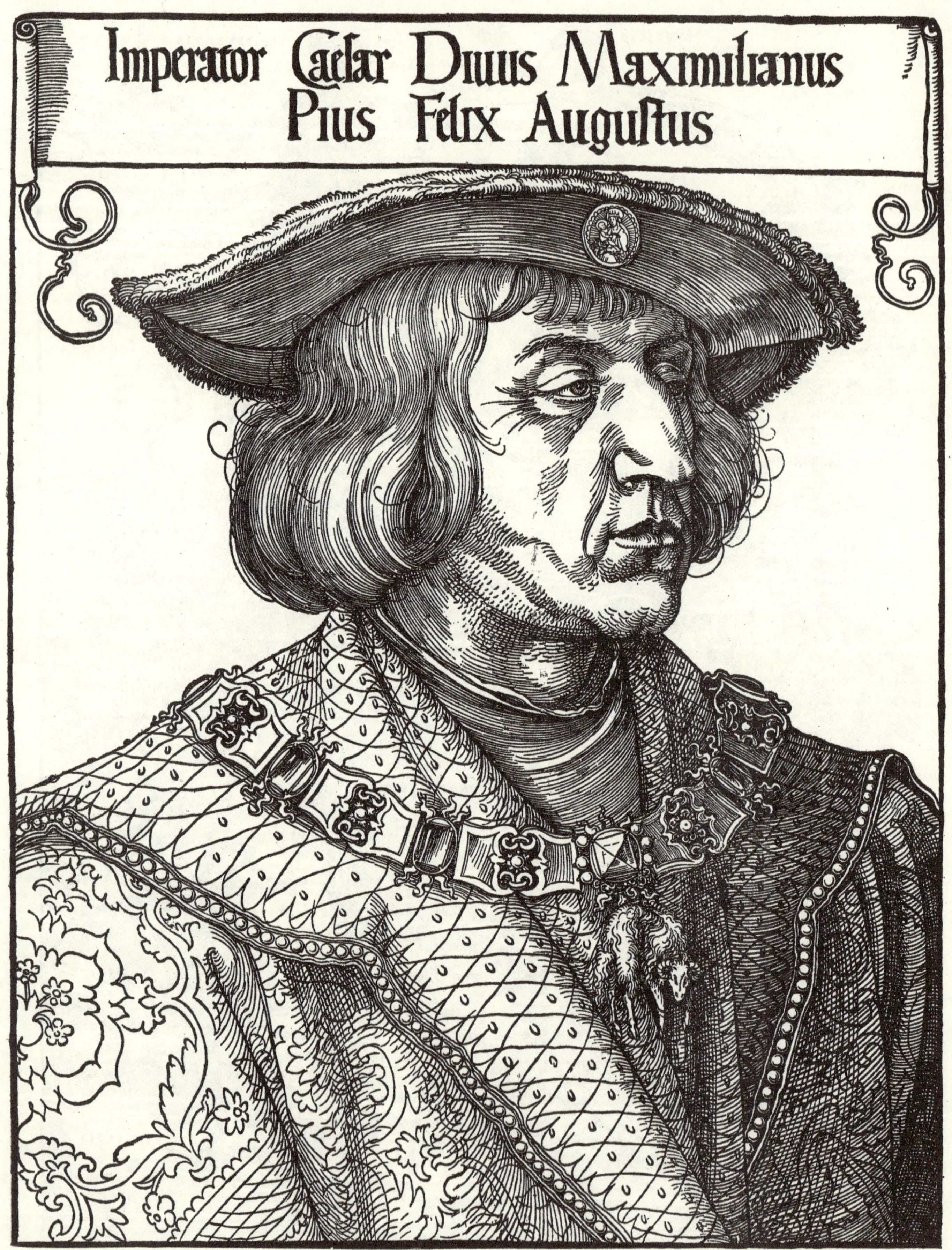

82. Portrait of the Emperor Maximilian

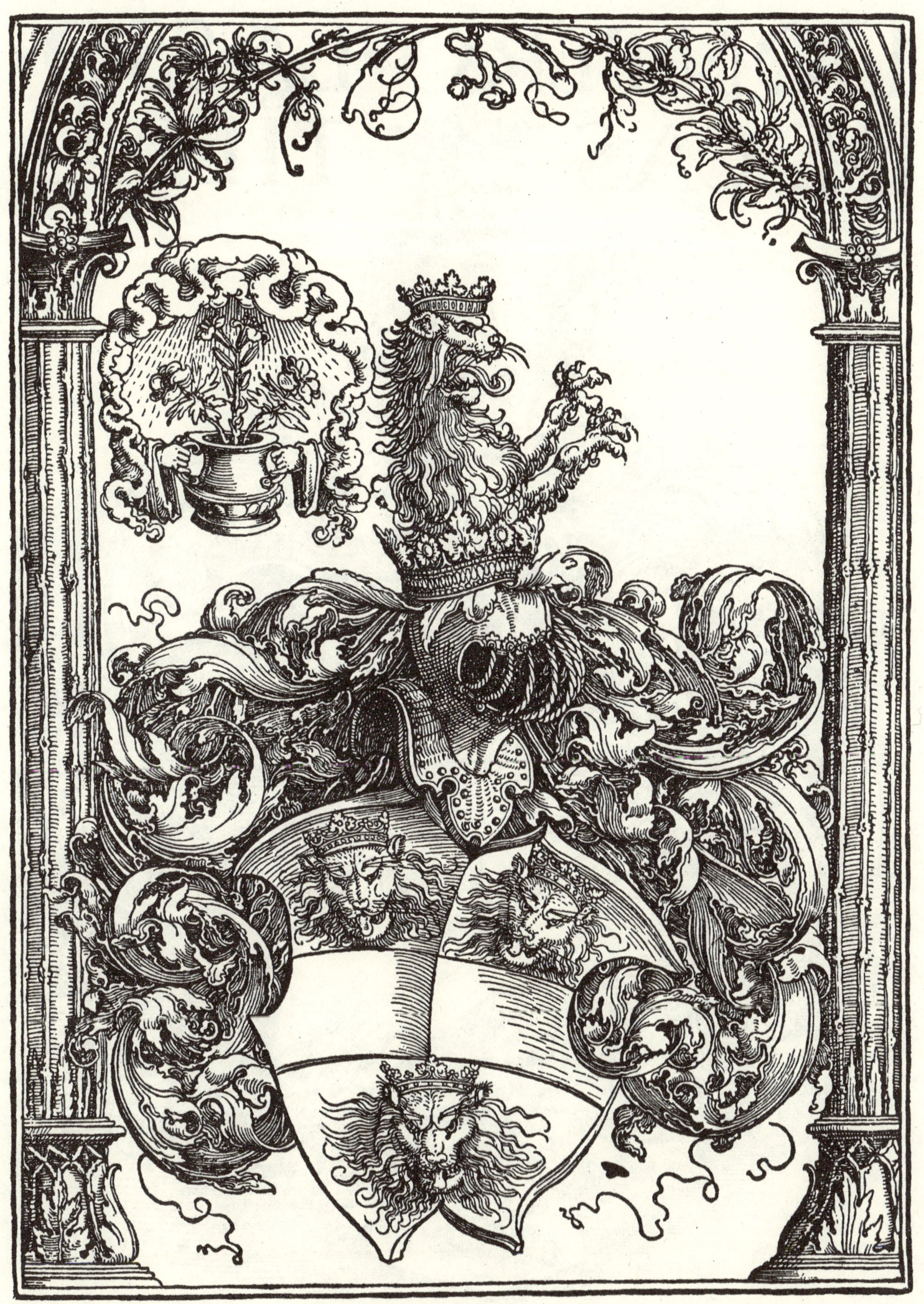

83. Coat of Arms with Three Lions' Heads

DON·PERO·LASSO·
DE·CAS TILLA·

84. Coat of Arms of Don Pedro Lasso

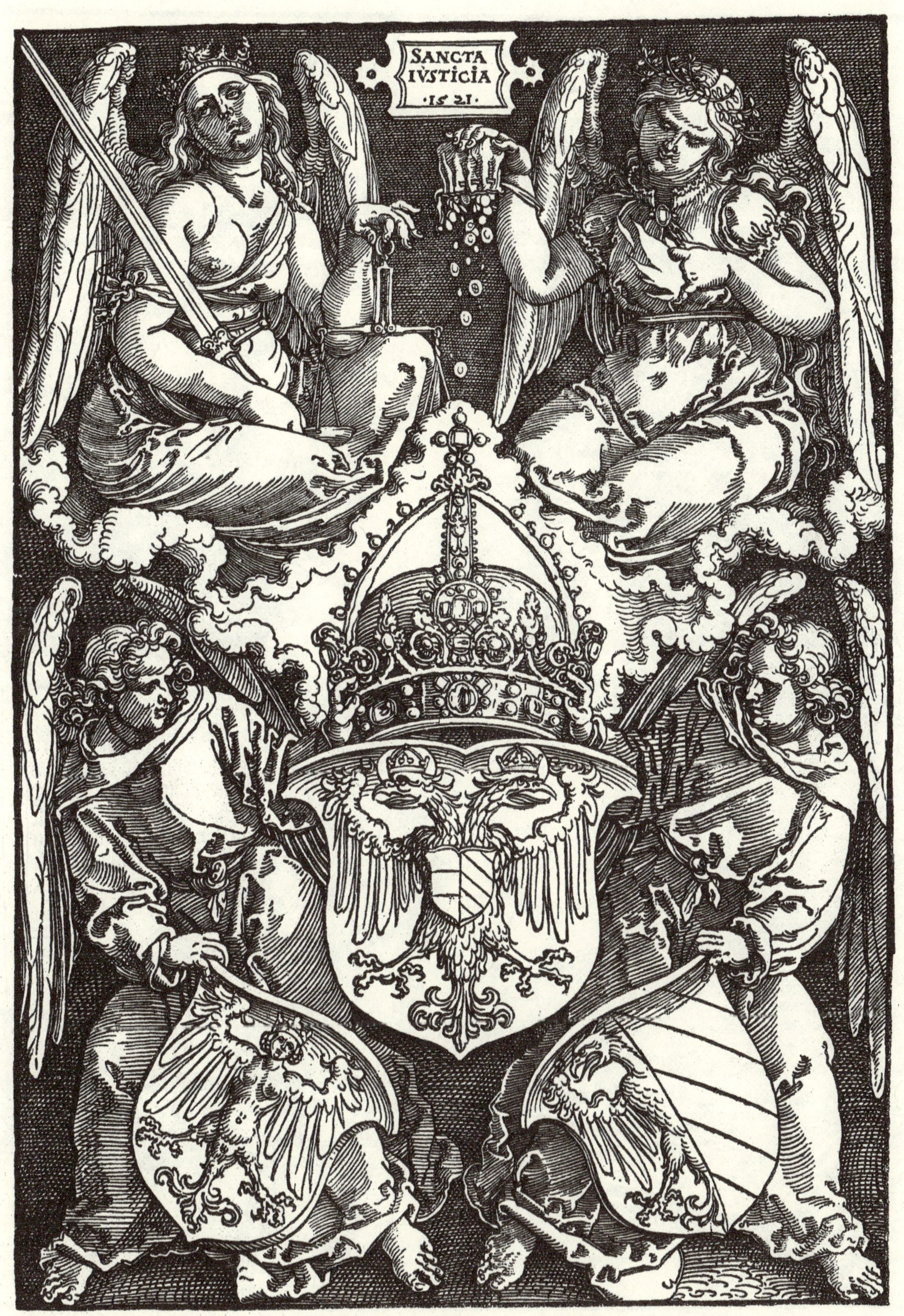

85. Coat of Arms of the Empire and of the City of Nuremberg

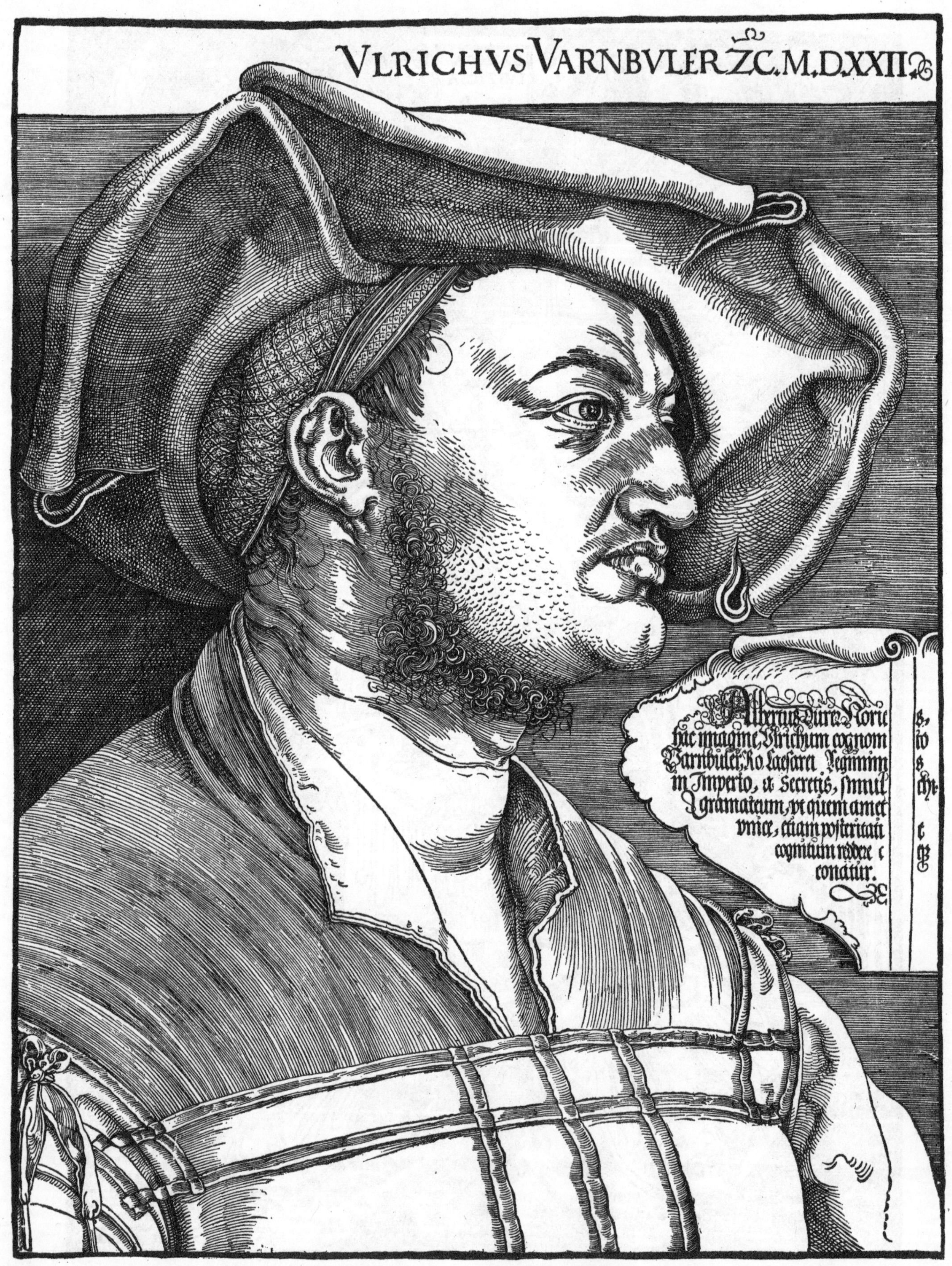

86. Portrait of Ulrich Varnbühler

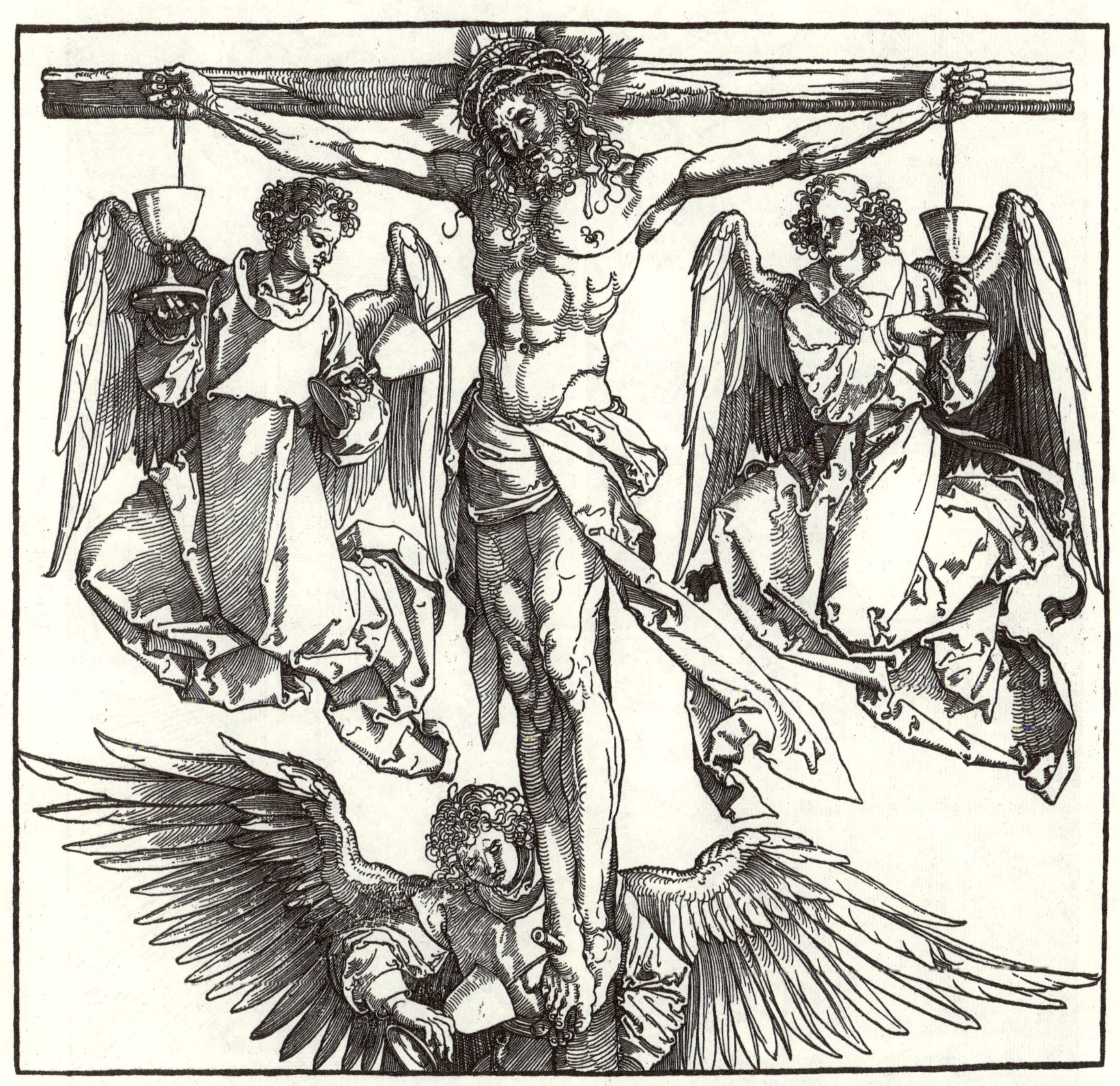

87. Christ on the Cross with Three Angels

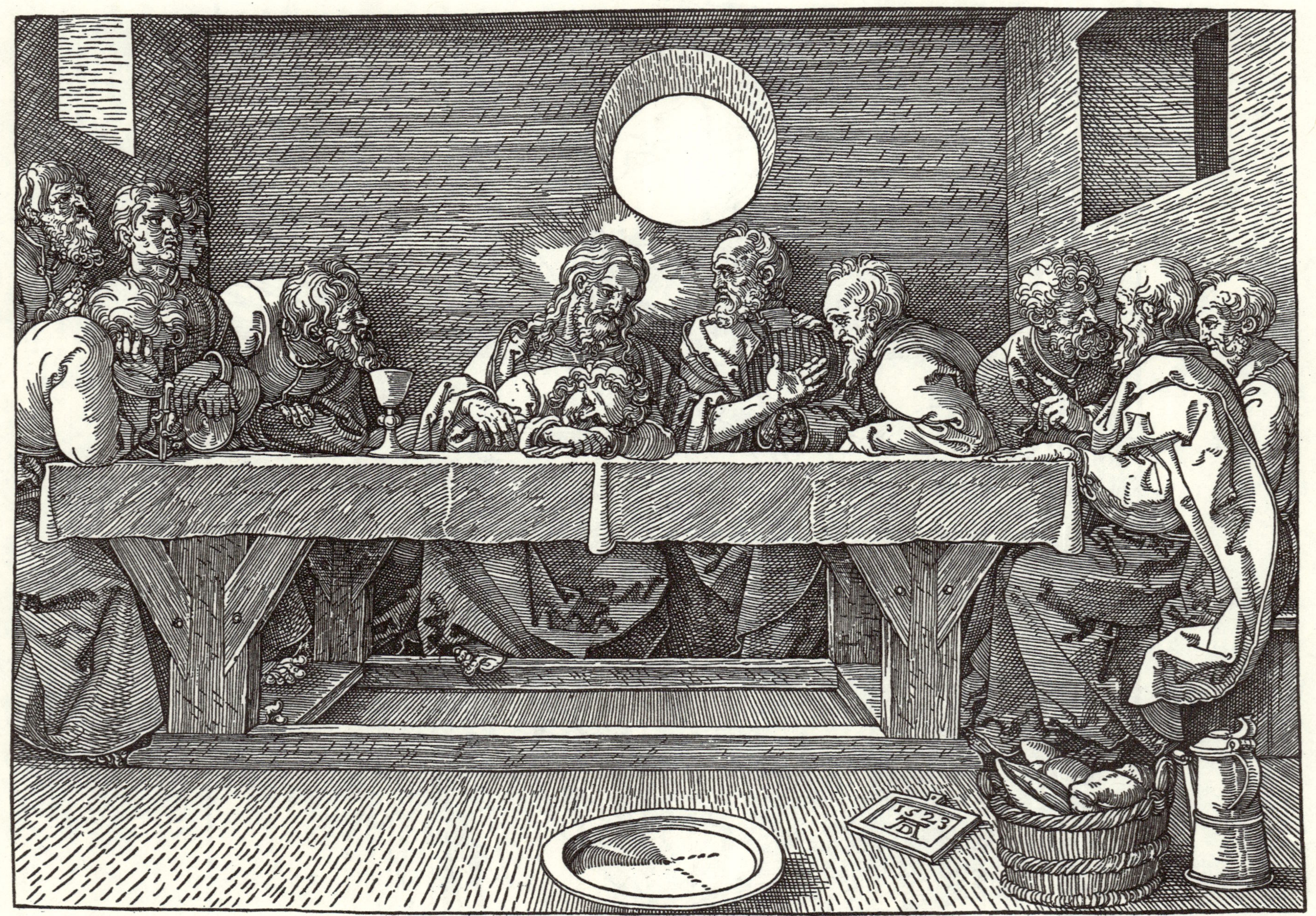

88. The Last Supper

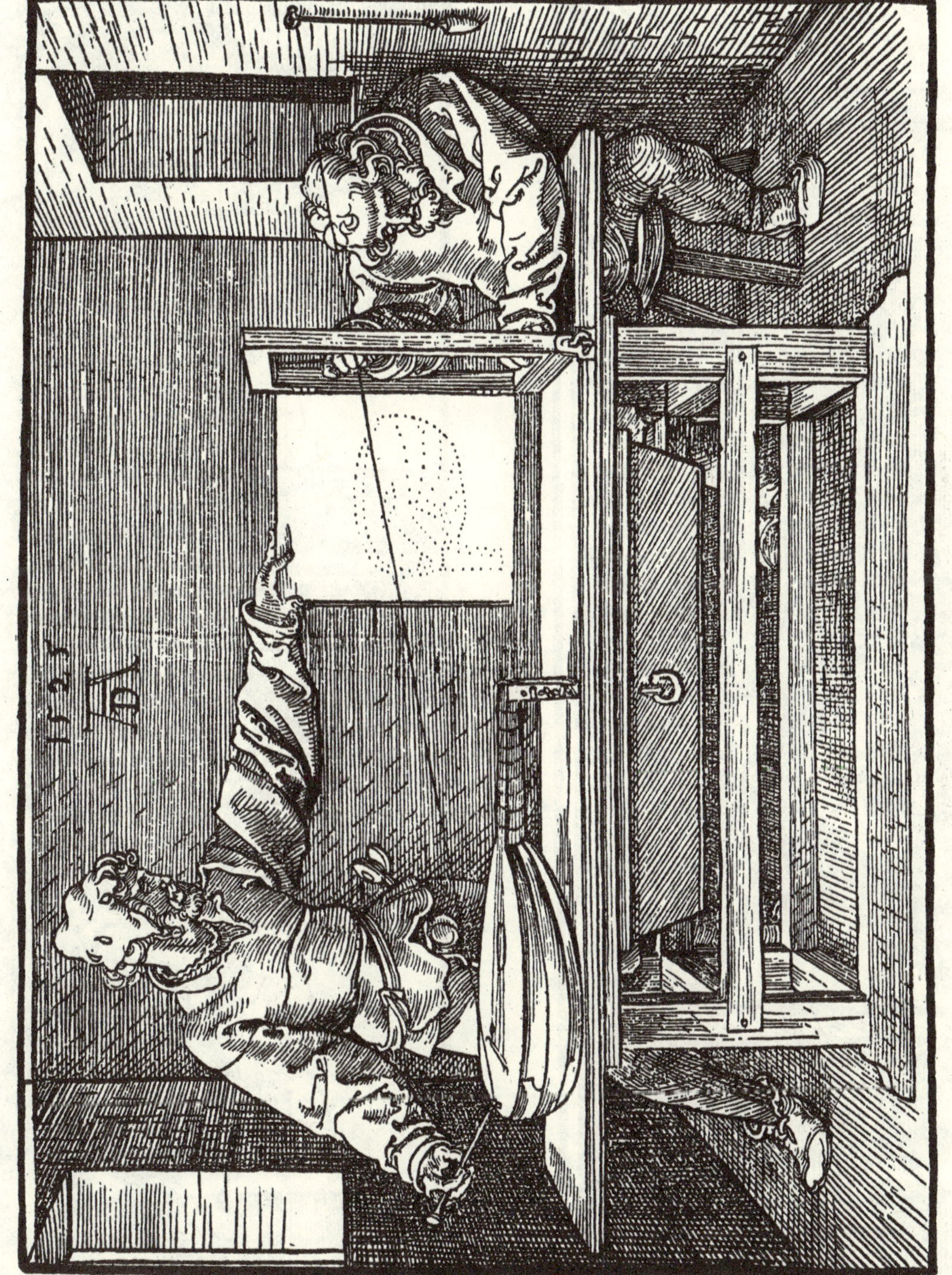

89. A man drawing a lute

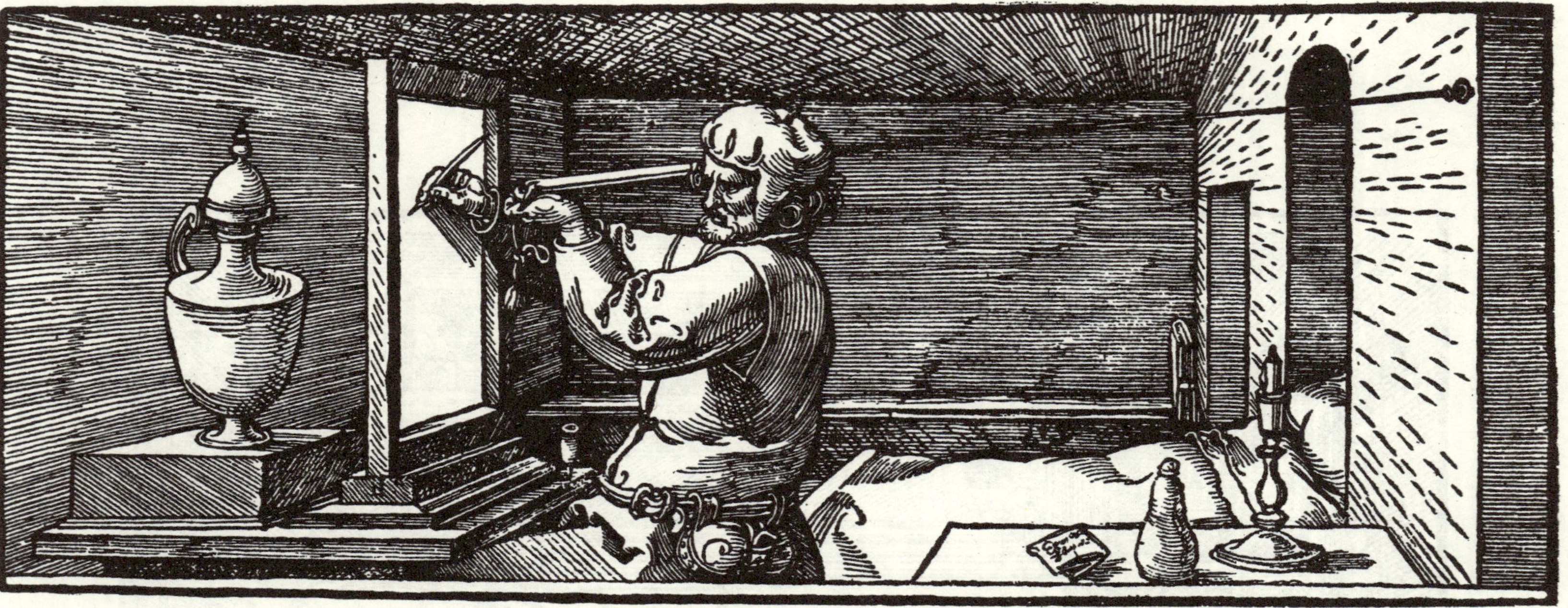

90. A man drawing a can

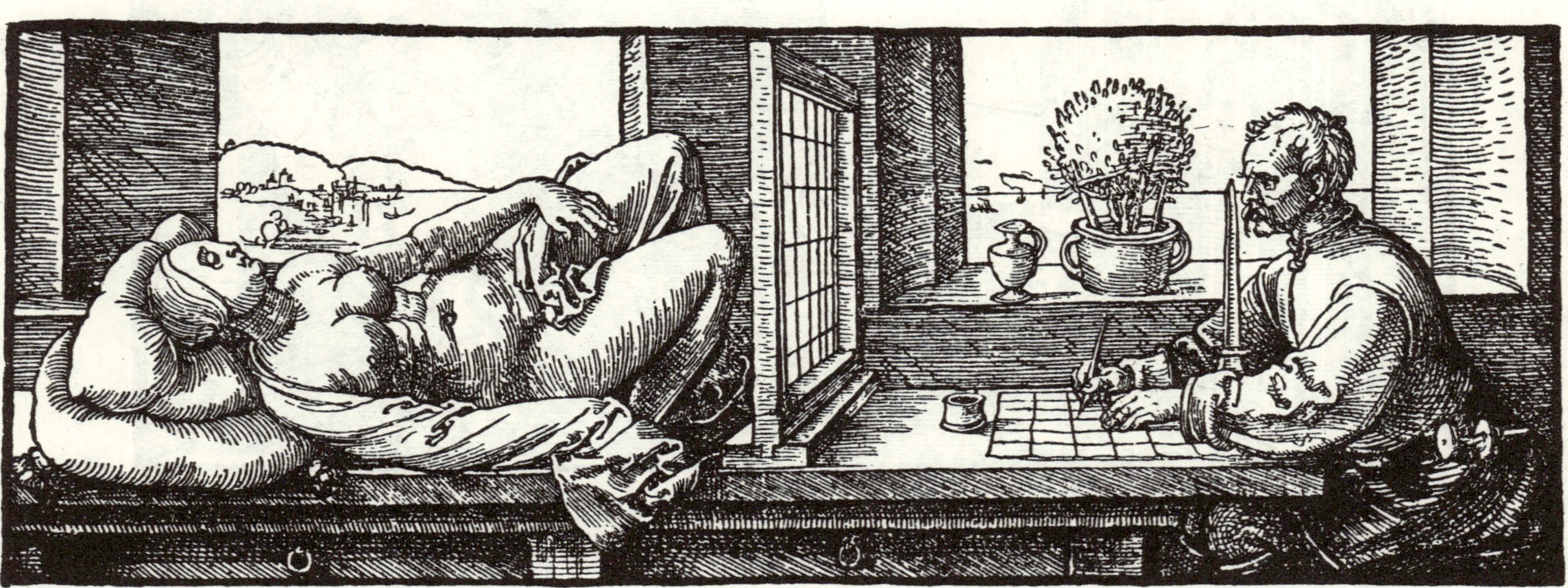

91. A man drawing a recumbent woman, in foreshortening through a frame with a network of squares

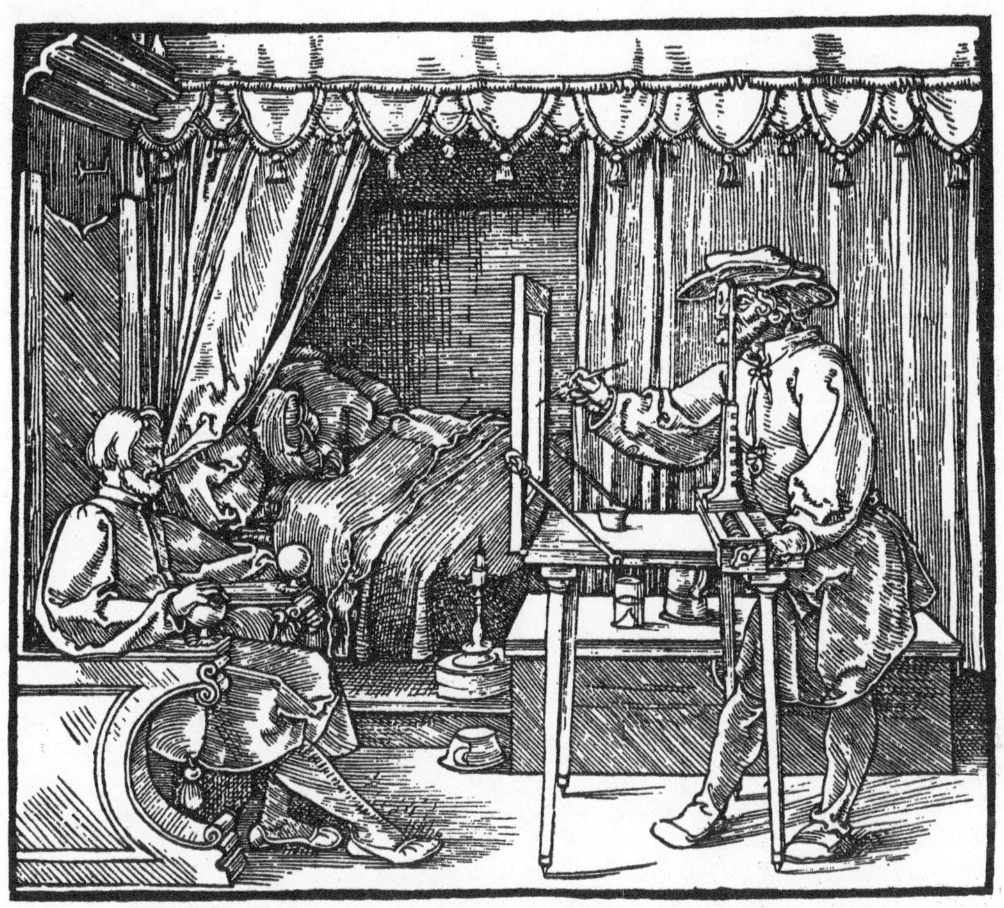

92. An artist drawing a seated man on to a pane of glass through a sight-vane

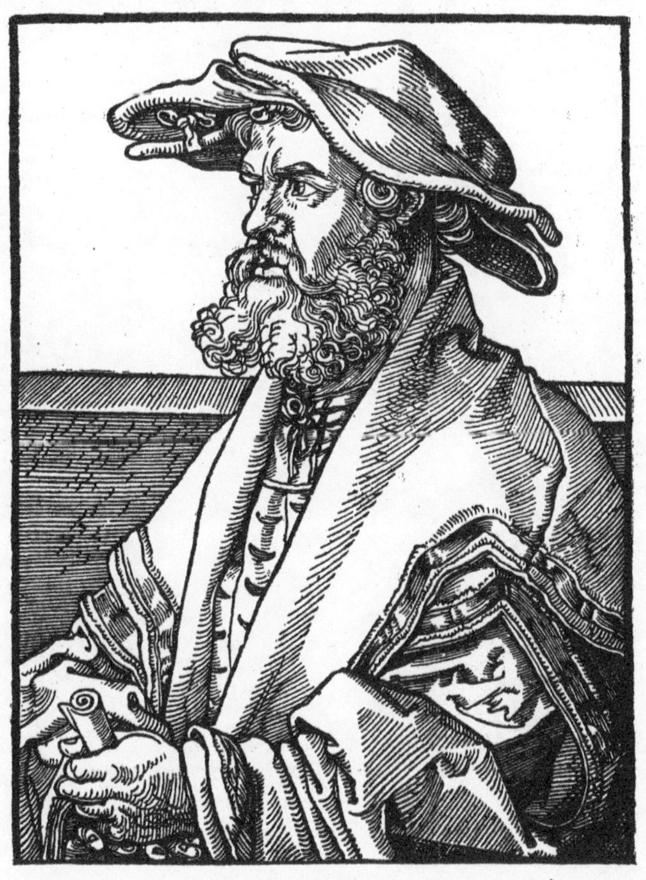

93. Portrait of Eobanus Hesse